To Johnny

Keep the Romance
in Love !

Manson xo

Illustrations by Graphic Designer | Michelle Beaudry
(www.beaudrystudio.com)

Cover Design by Graphic Designer | Michelle Beaudry
(www.beaudrystudio.com)

Book Design by Author | Colleen C. Carson

Editor | Colleen C. Carson

Co-Editing | Paloma Vita

Author's Photo | Photographer | Erik Zennstrom

www.theguyedbook.com

DEDICATION

Chance Kingsley Carson

February 20, 1984 – July 28, 2007

"I dedicate this book in memory of

Chance my adorable son

for his encouragement,

inspiration, and belief in me and

The Guyed Book.

Love you forever always my Angel."

THE GUYED BOOK

OUR STORY

"The Guyed Book" was borne when my teenaged son Chance was in high school. He asked me for some straightforward pointers on girls and romance. I started giving him advice, tips, and suggestions on the whys and how's of both.

My advice, tips, and suggestions were so effective that he asked me to write them down. The pages of advice eventually grew into an organized, secret "Guy-ed" book for Chance with a guy's mindset, "just tell me what to do" objective. Why a secret? We swore we would keep the book a secret because he didn't want anyone to know I was giving him advice, he wanted his friends to think it came naturally. Actually, he was a natural romantic since he was a little boy he just needed to understand how romance is the thank you in love.

Chance was very enthusiastic with the encouraging results. The young ladies comments were; "He's a keeper." "He listens to me." "He makes me feel very special." "He knows how to treat a woman." "He's so into me; he gets me." "He's so romantic." Chance not only used the tips, suggestions, and ideas when dating and in a relationship but with all the women in his life including me; he had an immense respect for women.

After Chance's sudden death on July 28th, 2007, I had this painful fear he would be forgotten. A legacy to remember him by was at the forefront of my thoughts, but what and how also existed, yet I knew that one day I would achieve this dream for him.

After his funeral, I made copies of our book and gave it to his best friends in memory of him. Then I put it away with all of his belongings forever, at least that's what I thought at the time.

Several years later, my daughter Crystal asked if she could send "The Guyed Book" to a friend. At first, I said no, but with her urging and my reluctance, I reviewed the book. I began to read all the while thinking about the fun, laughter, and words of encouragement we had shared together.

"THE GUYED BOOK" is a fun, straightforward self-help guide for guys on how to authentically triumph in romancing a woman. It worked for my son, and I know it will work for you. I know that Chance would love for me to share 'The GUYED BOOK' with the world as part of his legacy. Dreams do come true!

A percentage of book sales will be donated to "The Rise and Shine Foundation" in Chance's name.
www.theriseandshinefoundation.com

Thank
You

*"To my beautiful daughter Crystal
for her knowledge, motivation, and support.
Love you forever always!"*

(www.cncconsultinginc.com)

*"To Michelle Beaudry for her beautiful graphics,
talent, and the time she devoted, making this book
what I envisioned it to be."*

(www.beaudrystudio.com)

*"To Paloma Vita for your expertise in the
co-editing of my book."*

(www.palomavita.com)

*"To family and friends for their assistance and
encouragement in making my dream come true"*

AUTHOR

Colleen C. Carson lives on the west coast of Canada in the city of Vancouver. She's also a Mother, entrepreneur, image consultant, chef, event management specialist, writer, and now author.

She has been a lifelong romantic and a love enthusiast who, over the years, has been advising numerous men and women around the world on matters of the heart. Colleen believes that romance is the thank you in love, without it, love fades.

Whether it's a marriage gone awry or trying to survive and succeed the dating scene, Colleen has a comprehensive understanding of how relationships work (and why they don't). She has received praise from men and women around the world alike, for giving insight into love, romance, and dating.

She contributes her insight into love and romance based on her lifelong experiences, years of research, a marriage of 34 years, and herself navigating the dating scene for the last five years. Compassionate, open-minded, and easy to talk to she can hear what romantic hopefuls are wishing in their inner heart. A proponent of honesty above everything else, Colleen always gives a straight and honest answer, while being committed to making people come together in harmony.

TESTIMONIALS

"Your man may be perfect, but sometimes a little fine-tuning in the department of romance couldn't hurt. First-time author Colleen C. Carson takes a creative fun approach with her guidebook on love and romance written specifically for men, aptly titled The Guyed Book. The book base on Carson's experiences as well as those of her female and male friends filled with useful relationship pointers. The Guyed Book is a quick fun read with simple illustrations making it very guy friendly and something you can give him that doesn't resemble a volume of Emily Post -like rules."
Flare Online Magazine

My brother wanted help in learning more about women and romantic ideas, so he went to an expert; my Mom. Eventually Chance asked to have it put in book form, and The Guyed Book was created. Chance followed The Guyed Book and got rave reviews from the women in his life. Although written for guys to understand us women could definitely use it was well. It's informative, easy to absorb, fun, logical, and invaluable.
Crystal Carson | CNC Connections Agency | Vancouver

"The Guyed Book has really been great for me, and I have used it whether dating or in a relationship and got positive reactions. It worked for my Bro, Chance and now it works for me. I absolutely recommend this book for guys."
Randy Dilling |Chance's Best Friend | Vancouver

"Colleen has given us advice on how to be true, engaged and passionate about being together. She encourages us to be the best people we can be to one another and others around us. Her energy, intuitive personality allow for people to be open to her guiding them and nurturing their relationships. Colleen is a great person in our lives, and we are better for it."
Sharad and Nisha Kharé | Khare Communication

My fiancée and I read The Guyed Book which allowed me to 'plant the seed' of intention without sounding nagging or "why don't you do this for me" tone. The Guyed Book is a fun and creative romance activity book for both men and women. Colleen has hit romance 'out of the park'! We loved the interaction we shared together while reading The Guyed Book.
Cindy Tran | Vancouver

"Spending time with Colleen reminds me that real life is simple if we live by the truth. I so value her, and her insight! Colleen's words and advice are brilliant, true and so very wise. She never sugar coats it and always tells it like it is, how it should be and how to do it. She listens without judgment, and I walk away a better partner, friend, and more inspired woman."
Chelsea McDonald | Animal Technician | Vancouver

"Colleen has given me the opportunity to see love from a different perspective. Many times we are blinded by our own beliefs, missing the opportunity to fall in love and true passion on our everyday activities. What I have experienced after speaking to her, is that she has a unique sensibility to point out on people the missing links that might be needed to experience the full benefits of the power of love. Thank you, Colleen, for committing to such a wonderful endeavor."
Paulino Suarez | Producer | Actor | Mexico City

"Colleen, or 'Mama Carson' as she is called by me and my friends, is a warm, intuitive, and thoughtful soul. She has real experience and a deep knowledge of how men and women relate to each other in matters of the heart. Her advice is always honest and kind."
JN-Publicist | Los Angeles, CA

"Colleen has an extremely unique gift in that she is effortlessly able to recognize and articulate what is going on beneath the surface, be it in matters of health, romance, work or relationships. She is incredibly easy to

talk to, and her advice is always thoughtful and honest. She is a tender soul that has the ability to enlighten those who are in need of guidance or unbiased advice."
Meghan Brush | Sales Representative | Vancouver

"Colleen tells it like it is. She sees the very best in me and therefore only wants the best for me. She has accurately called out why certain relationships didn't work out in the past and has accurately called out the kind of man that is the fit for me. Not the perfect man, but the kind who fits. Even if I start to entertain the idea of the "Mr. right now", she quickly sees it and reminds me of my worth. Her compassion, yet directness makes Colleen the ideal relationship coach."
Patricia | Actress | Los Angeles

"Colleen is always honest in her advice; she shows the guidance that we couldn't see by ourselves."
Eve C.| Lawyer | São Paulo, Brazil

"Colleen has walked with me through my make-ups, break-ups, new relationships and times of pain. She is honest, intuitive and knowledgeable, especially when it comes to matters of the heart. Colleen has years of experience which brings a certain wisdom and strength that a textbook cannot teach. Her words are empowering and meaningful and will leave you truly inspired."
A. Naidoo | Councilor | Vancouver

"Colleen is one of the warmest most thoughtful people I know. She had given me unforgettable insights into love and life...time and time again."
Matt Cantor | Producer and DJ | London, England

"As long as I have known Colleen I have come to her for relationship advise. She is caring, intelligent and insightful and has an ability to see a situation from my perspective. Colleen will tell you deep down what your heart already knows, but you need to hear from someone with experience."
Cara T | Event Planner | Melbourne, Australia

WARNING:

This book is not for the weak of heart
18+ suggested reader
all genders welcome
controversy in the making
out-of-the box thinking
the truth exposed
this read guarantees
YOU
romantic success

Sensuality + Sexuality = Romance

"Romance is the thank you in Love!"

Colleen Carson

PREFACE

My knowledge has come from 34 years of marriage, along with many friends and family members over the years who came to me for relationship advice and romantic tips. And of course presently, my dating experiences over the last five years.

I have come to recognize the one aspect of our lives we can't do without is love. We have a love of family and friends, but the love we are in search of is the everlasting love between a man and woman. I remember a friend saying to me, "I will search wherever I can to find love... I can't live without it."

Love is intoxicating; it brings such powers of joy, fascination, and exhilaration. Love at the beginning of a relationship is known as romantic love, what follows is what I call Established Love. What I have learned over the years is that as Established Love grows, we tend to give less importance to our Romantic Love.

Life happens, but what undermines your relationship is making excuses for why you have allowed your love to lessen in importance because of outside influences and priorities.

Love alone will not survive. Over the decades, the couples who survived the difficulties in their relationship were the same ones who combined both established love and romantic love with equal importance and admiration allowing the inevitable of Everlasting Love.

TABLE OF CONTENTS

PLANNED EVENTS

A FARE CHANCE

INTRODUCTION

"The Guyed Book" it's informative, effective and results driven with relationship pointers, tips, ideas, recipes, and events on romance purposely written for guys (that women can find useful as well.

I.   THE WOMAN

Sensuality V Sexuality: Intimacy is sensuality, whereas sex is sexuality; Successful romantic relationships include a balance of both. Women are about sensuality and guys are about sexuality.
Romantic & Established Love: Romantic love is the "Butterflies" at the beginning of a relationship. Established love is the acceptance of the best of us to the less of us without judgment.
The 17 Official Grievances: Typical complaints that women have in relationships. For example, "manners are foreign to him" and "let me know if you're going to be late."
The Mystery of She: A questionnaire about their partner. For example, "What are her sexual fantasies?"

II.   THE GUY

Communication: Includes the eight fundamentals of successful communication (clarity, positivity, respectfulness, open-ended questions, body language, voice tone, attitude, and listening) and the "L.I.S.T.E.N." acronym.
Gentlemen's Commandments: This is all about Chivalry. For example, "Thou shalt be loyal" and "Thou shalt be polite."
Guys Styling: Outlines four fashion styles for men: gallant, urbane, youthful and stylish.
Dating Advice: What 30 dating pointers create appeal? Such as learning about her interests, and keeping your cell phone on silent.

Did You Know: Fun facts about love and romance; did you know that the oldest sex manual was published in China 5,000 years ago? These questions have two purposes to them; starting an interesting conversation, and getting to know you:

The "MR" Factor: The eight principals of the "MR" factor that will leave her powerless.

III.   ROMANTIC CONNECTION

The language of Love: Includes a list of love adjectives and steps on how to properly compliment a woman and more.

Flower Sense: Outlines the symbolism of various flowers (i.e. Daisies represent innocence and purity).

Bedazzle Her: Outlines different birthstones and gemstones.

Romantic Accents: Lists accessories that add a romantic ambiance to a room, such as music and lighting.

Romantic Gifts: Suggestions for romantic gifts; perfume or a spa day.

Top 30 Author Song Picks: List of romantic tunes.

101 Magical Moments: Lists romantic gestures someone can do for their partner.

IV.   PLANNED EVENTS

Garden of Love: Instructions on how to create a customized "Garden of Love" for one's partner.

Car Wash: Instructions on how to do a surprise car wash for your partner, with a romantic finishing touch.

The Calendar: Instructions on how to create an activity calendar for one's partner.

Our Date Night: Instructions on how to organize the perfect date night.

Christmas in July: Instructions on how to plan a Christmas celebration for your partner, with gift suggestions and décor ideas.

Queen for a Day: Instructions on how to plan a day of pampering for your partner, including a timeline and organizational tips.

V. A FARE CHANCE

Culinary Sensuality: A list of sensual foods enhancing the seductive aspect of dining.

Table Setting for Home Dining: Instructions on how to properly set a formal dinner table.

Dining Ambiance: Creating a romantic setting while dining at home.

Wine Pairing: Price ranges, varietals, glassware and temperature of wines from various regions.

Food Portions: Portion sizes for men and women's entrees and desserts.

Dinner Centerpiece: Offers centerpiece arrangement suggestions for the dinner table (i.e. classic white, dramatic, themed piece and last-minute ideas).

A Romantic Affare: Suggests a date night menu that includes the shopping list and cooking instructions.

Twilight Picnic: Suggestions of how to arrange a romantic picnic date, including recipes and musical accompaniment.

Italian My Love: A homemade pizza is having your partner's name or a message spelled out using a variety of pizza toppings.

The Hearty Brunch: Recipes on heart shaped food creating a romantic ambiance.

A Fare Chance Mini Cookbook: Extra delicious recipes.

Sensuality + Sexuality = Romance

THE
WOMAN

"AS MY BODY LAID AGAINST HIS I IN THOUGHT OF HIS MAGNIFICENCE
JOYFUL IN THE PULSE OF OUR LOVE US ETCHED IN MY HEART FOREVER."

SENSUALITY V **SEXUALITY**

Women are about sensuality and guys are about sexuality. What's the difference between sensuality and sexuality? Sensuality is the desire of the senses; sight, scent, taste, touch, and sound. Sexuality is the action of a person's desires; sexual intercourse. Consequently, embrace sensuality with sexuality and you have intimacy, not sex.

Women are consistent in using all their senses to act, bond, and develop their feelings and sexual experience, I call this sensuality. It's not that guys don't use their senses; you do but not with the intensity of importance and not all your senses at one time. Women bring sensuality into their sexual experience to attain their want for a romantic experience.

What is romance? Romance is the thank you in love. Women need a thank you for their love, and some men as well. I would say women outnumber the men for the want and need of romance in their relationship. Why, because guys are about sexuality. Guys think of sex as they do food and sleep. Guys need, and women want sexual activity, but for the woman, sex becomes more enjoyable when sensually is involved.

Generally speaking guy's think of sex as having sex, women think of sex as making love, intimacy. I'm not talking about the one night stand - in that case, both have the need for sex - there is no sensuality, just sex on both parts.

Let's start at the beginning: a man and woman meeting for the first time and they have chemistry. What then? Okay, this is where it can get a little confusing. I had heard women say, "When we first met, he was very romantic!" Does this mean your sensuality was at the same level as your sexuality hence romance?

It's quite complimentary if you think about it, she acknowledges that you are capable of sensuality. The trouble is you weren't aware of it; your awareness was the quest of this woman and a possible relationship. Again the difference; women are aware of their sensuality, and guys are not.

I believe men are sensual, but awareness is the key. When you have the existence of both sensuality and sexuality, you will create a romantic ambiance.

An example of romance using the five senses:

- The scent of an alluring fragrance
- The vision of an adoring poise
- The sound of a suggestive voice
- The touch of a loving embrace
- The taste of a sensuous kiss

Be appreciative of your senses, and she will be in awe of you. By the way, romance is not always about candlelight dinners, roses, and caviar taste.

Romance can be the simplest of simple things, like holding hands. Also, Romance has never been about how much money you spend, it's always about the thoughtful gestures, and moments you create with the thought of bringing happiness to your special someone.

ROMANTIC & ESTABLISHED LOVE

What is love? I believe this question has been asked over and over again through the decades even centuries and the definitions are numerous. Maybe because there are many facets of love from feelings, actions, intimacy, wants and needs, unconditional, and conditional that forms a relationship between a man and a woman.

Let's begin with the coupling stages of love; Romantic and Established, each stage should enhance the other. These stages determine in the relationship whether you will be lovers or life partners, but first, let me explain the meaning of love as I see it.

Love is both a noun and verb. The noun (person) of love is the passionate feeling of affection; the verb (action) is the showing your appreciation of that feeling. Simply put whether it's touching, acknowledgment, sharing time, the doing or giving in recognition of your love to each other, both have to take action through a form of expression to have growth in your relationship and confirmation of your love. The feeling is beautiful the action is essential and equal.

There's an old saying that I grew up hearing and it refers to love; "Women need to be told, and men need to be shown." I took it for the truth, but in my journeys of love I can say with no hesitation, it goes both ways.

What about wants or needs of love? What's the difference? Want is a desire, need is a necessity. I believe the wants and needs of love within a relationship can allow for growth, but they must stay balanced. Once a person needs more than wants you to have enslavement, as with wants more than needs you have autonomy, either without balance will eventually end your love and the relationship. What is conditional and unconditional love? Very simply; conditional love has conditions, and unconditional love does not. Yes, of course, I'll explain what I mean.

Your inner child plays a poignant role in this aspect. The inner child is the part of your psyche believed to retain feelings as experienced in childhood before puberty. If raised by a parent's whose love is of blame and shame, you know of conditional love. Raised by parent's whose love is of acceptance and respect, you know of unconditional love.

I believe that when in love know what type of relationship your woman has with her parents, and vice versa. Let me explain, the first relationship of love we have in life is with our parents hence our inner child. The relationship she has with the opposite gender parent is the relationship she will have with you. The relationship she has with her same gender parent will be a reflection of the love she expresses.

I have explained love as both a noun meaning emotions and a verb meaning actions. I believe awareness of each other's way of love will be the longevity of the relationship. I have heard people say if it's true love you shouldn't have to work at it. You shouldn't have to work at love, but you do have to put effort into the relationship for it to grow.

I have met couples that loved and adored each other, yet eventually, their relationship ended, and the reason is the effort in making a relationship a healthy and vibrant one was minimal or maybe too different. An example; you fall in love with someone who only knows of conditional love, and you're about unconditional love. Will your relationship survive the difference? Yes, but you'll both have to invest a lot of effort into the understanding of your differences through communication, honesty, trust, action, and patience.

What is Romantic Love? When a relationship begins with chemistry, it will rapidly develop into Romantic love. Romantic love is the intimacy of sensuality and sexuality. Romantic love is that feeling of butterflies with the thought of the other; it's exhilarating, fascinating, and takes your breath away with excitement. If that's all you want to feel, then you will continue to experience many beginnings and ends in relationships. Hey if that makes you happy then go for it!

What is Established Love? It's the love that follows after the romantic love, the learning of each other; the flaws, failures, annoyances, good, bad and every little secret. I will say with confidence both these loves equally embraced in practice will form a lasting love until death do us part.

I believe guys can be equally sensitive and romantic as women, but they must utilize their senses to achieve the same goal. Societies both past and even present profess guys have to be stronger emotionally than females. My answer to that is; Why? Women have told me when their man shows sensitivity; it's an intimate moment of revelation of tenderness.

Honesty   **Harmony**

Inspiration   **Elation**

Senses   **Romance**

I believe both genders are equal emotionally at birth; the change in our emotions begins during puberty where the influences of our social environment and society's expectations reared its restrictive reign of beliefs.

We all have a masculine and feminine thought process, which we can choose to recognize or ignore. When recognizing we develop an understanding, along with our senses the acceptance of love being equally emotional in action and reaction to each other.

THE 17 OFFICIAL GRIEVANCES

1. Say what you mean, mean what you say.
2. A promise is about keeping it.
3. He doesn't listen to me.
4. I want a man, not a boy.
5. I don't feel appreciated.
6. Chivalry is foreign to him.
7. He doesn't know how to have fun.

8. I'm always taking the lead.
9. I want romance in our relationship.
10. His priorities always come first.
11. He's turned into such a slob.
12. Frugal is one thing, cheap is another.
13. My time is just as valuable as yours
14. I think his friends are more important than me.
15. I feel like he doesn't care what my interests are.
16. He's a mama's boy.
17. He rarely ever compliments me.

THE MYSTERY OF SHE

I would write a whole page on why it's imperative for you to do this questionnaire with your special someone. Instead, I will give you a somewhat familiar scenario of a conversation a couple may have...

Guy: Hey, Hon, where would you like to go for dinner tonight?

Girl: Oh, I don't know.

Guy: What type of food are you thinking?

Girl: Actually, I wasn't.

Guy: What are you in the mood for?

Girl: Don't know.

Guy: Okay, is there a favourite restaurant?

Girl: No, not really. Babe, you surprise me. *("Just plan dinner, OMG take the lead.")*

Guy: So, you haven't got any ideas? What about the restaurant on Violet that just opened a couple of months ago? *("I hate when she does this, why can't she just tell me?")*

Girl: What restaurant is that?

Guy: I can't remember the name, but I think it's a Thai restaurant.

Girl: Hmmm!

Guy: What's wrong I thought you liked Thai food?

Girl: It's okay, but not tonight. *("Are you serious, I eat it because it's one of your favourite foods.")*

Guy: Okay. *("She told me she wasn't thinking of any type of food.")*

Girl: I trust you in arranging dinner.

Guy: I think I know where you would like to go, just leave it to me. *("I don't get why she wants to put us through this misery, whatever I do I know it's going to be wrong.")*

Hours later they're off for dinner, both excited about the evening. Conversation is light and fun.

Guy: I hope you enjoy this evening I really thought about you when I planned tonight. *("Let's hope I got this right.")*

Girl: Awe, thank you, baby, I knew you could do it. *("Let's hope he got it right.")*

They arrive and enter the restaurant; he looks at her and knows...

Okay Guys, raise your hand if you've experienced this or something similar? Unhappy situations only occur because of lack of information. Hence, the questionnaire; problem solver!

The questions are designed to get you to know her. By the way, many of the questions are for couples in a committed relationship, but there are questions when dating as well, those are in the red. Suggestion for a little fun take turns asking each other the questions; it's informative and maybe even surprising.

1. Birthdate?
2. Significant dates we've shared?
3. A favourite romantic experience?
4. Favourite nickname?
5. Described a fantasy date?
6. Describe an anniversary idea?
7. Do you like surprises?
8. Favourite season of the year?
9. Favourite holiday celebration?
10. Favourite time of the day?
11. Favourite day of the week?
12. Favourite personal activities?
13. Favourite activity on a rainy or winter day:
    Reading
    Cuddling
    Baking
    Lunch
    Movie
    Gym
    Shopping
14. Favourite activity on a hot sunny day?
    Sunbathe
    Beach
    Barbeque

Outdoor Venture
Boating
15. Style of fashion preferred? Define?
Classic
Romantic
Dramatic
Sporty
Creative
Trendy
Natural
16. Favourite colors in clothing?
17. Clothing patterns preferred?
Floral
Plaid
Stripe
Solid
Sparkle
18. Favourite sleepwear? Size?
Pajamas
Nightgown
Lingerie
Chemise
Sleep Shirt
Teddy
19. Shoe size?
20. Style of footwear preferred?
Sneaker
Sandal
Stiletto
Platform
Flat
Boot
Flip Flops
Slipper
21. Bra size?
22. Panty size?

23. Blouse/Sweater size?
24. Dress size?
25. Pant size?
26. Dress suit size?
27. Favourite colour/s?
28. Preferred flower/s?
29. Favourite flower colour?
30. Favourite gem/stones?
31. The fashion of jewelry preferred?
32. Gold or silver jewelry preference?
33. What are your Cosmetic needs?
    Face
    Eyes
    Lips
    Eyebrows
34. Body and face creams preferred?
35. Facial cleansing products preferred?
36. Manicures and Pedicures preferred?
37. Favourite nail polish colours?
38. Favourite hair products?
39. Personal hairstylist's name?
40. Favourite Hair products?
41. Name of your personal spa?
42. Beauty treatments preferred?
43. Favourite perfume/s?
44. What type of fitness preferred?
    Gym
    Team Sport
    Yoga
    Roller Blading
    Running
    Swimming
45. Prefer to play and watch sports?
46. Which sports?
47. Favourite hobbies?
48. What books do you prefer?

49. Favourite poet?
50. Types of movies preferred?
51. Favourite television shows?
52. Selection of music preferred?
53. Favourite entertainers/performers?
54. Do you like camping and lodging?
55. Do you like traveling? Where?
56. Favourite travel spot/s?
57. Favourite season you prefer to travel?
58. Do you prefer dining in or dining out? Why?
59. Favourite cuisine?
60. Favourite restaurant?
61. Favourite candy/chocolate?
62. Favourite junk food?
63. Preferred cocktail drink?
64. Favourite wine?
65. Favourite beer?
66. What fashion style do you prefer on me?
67. Favourite men's cologne?
68. Prefer topics of conversation?
69. When stressed what type of support do you appreciate?
70. What type of communication skills do you prefer?
71. Favourite couple activities?
72. Favourite couple massages?
73. Favourite time of day for making love?
74. Describe a sensuous evening for two?
75. What part of foreplay do you enjoy the most?
76. Would you engage in a truth and dare bedroom game?
77. Would you enjoy going sex toy shopping?
78. What are your erogenous zones?
79. What are your sexual fantasies?
80. What are your sexual fetishes?

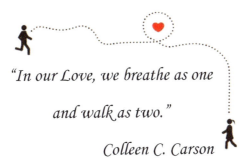

"In our Love, we breathe as one

and walk as two."

Colleen C. Carson

THE GUY

"BOTH HEARTS WELCOME THE UNKNOWN WORDS OF AFFECTION
NURTURE BY JOY ROMANTIC MOMENTS OF ENDLESS PLEASURE
WHILST HIS LOVE GIVES DAWN TO HERS."

COMMUNICATION

Listen
In
Silence
To
Express
Notions

Communication is the lifeline of a healthy and vibrant relationship. When your partner has something to express, make it a priority to listen, because left unexpressed could lead to resentment and a possibility of an eventual demise of your relationship.

Your partner must know that their feelings are foremost in your priorities; when they need to discuss their thoughts, you must acknowledge their importance by listening to them.

When conveying your thoughts, the following eight fundamentals must come into play to have the most positive result:

1. Clarity – stick to the point and be transparent.
2. Positivity – keep communication encouraging.
3. Respectful – no blame game, express your feelings on the both of you.
4. Open ended questions – avoid a simple yes or no

to the question.

5. Body Language – keep eye contact, open posture, not in their space and put the cell phone away or any other distraction.

6. Voice Tone – make it welcoming when conveying or responding.

7. Attitude – be part of the solution not part of the problem.

8. Listen – don't interrupt, the same letters in listen are also in the word silent.

Men and women both believe someone should be right well the other is wrong; why does there have to be a right or wrong? How could it feel good about making the one you love to feel bad? Considering that we are all different yet similar in our opinions and approaches, we must communicate within reason for the other to understand and accept what we have to say. There will be times to agree to disagree but first and foremost, always respect each other's opinion. The importance of what you have to communicate to each other is equal in importance and should be valued with the same effort.

GENTLEMAN'S COMMANDMENTS

I have discovered that guys are interested in wanting to be chivalrous, and women although independent and self-reliant want their man to treat them like a lady in an old fashion sense. The problem is the ordinary guy has a vague idea of what chivalry is, and women think they have to prove their independence continuously. Give yourselves all a break; if a woman wants a man in her life, then she will have to allow him to treat her like a lady.

Ladies, chivalry does not take away your independence nor your confidence. A real man will always appreciate your independence and admire your confidence. When you're truly confident and independent, you don't need to prove it. I'm a confident and independent woman, but I also want the luxury of being treated like a lady. So, what's wrong with that?

- Thou shalt be loyal
- Thou shalt be polite
- Thou shalt be honest
- Thou shalt be sincere
- Thou shalt open doors
- Thou shalt be attentive
- Thou shalt be respectful
- Thou shalt arrive on time
- Thou shalt never interrupt
- Thou shalt honour thy word
- Thou shalt defend her honour
- Thou shalt dress in a pleasing way
- Thou shalt always respect her intellect
- Thou shalt state please and thank you
- Thou shalt grant her entry and exit first
- Thou shalt be attentive to her schedule
- Thou shalt bestow sincere compliments
- Thou shalt be courteous with generosity
- Thou shalt assist her in and out of her coat
- Thou shalt assist her in and out of her chair
- Thou shalt walk on the outside of the street
- Thou shalt escort her to her door of residence

GUYS STYLING

GALLANT

URBANE

YOUTHFUL

STYLISH

Hey Guys, styling yourself is important if you wish to be successful whether in your private or business life. If you are capable of achieving this yourself or need to hire someone to assist you, it's imperative you get it right.

You know how women speak of that little black dress. Why is the little black dress essential in our wardrobe? Black is a color that hides all flaws, it personifies sophistication and confidence, and you can change the look by accessorizing. Well guys, for you the black suit, every man young and old should have one, for all the same reasons. When a man accessorizes his suit its all about the shirt, tie, and pocket square. Whether the shirt has a design or solid in color, it will change the message you're trying to give. You should also have in your wardrobe a pair of black dress shoes to wear with the black suit.

When it comes to styling; the empower man and adventurous boy should be reflected. It's about styling your personality; it doesn't have to take half your income to achieve this goal and look good.

Example: A boyfriend of two years had a wardrobe that was 20 years old. On occasion, he would add something minor to it, but it was rare. He always looked appealing, sexy and confident.

Why? He took the time to learn about his fashion style to reflect his personality, which covered his flaws and exposed his attributes while reflecting his confidence.

I wonder what some of you are thinking when you dress for an outing with a woman. Women will spend hours thinking through what they should wear for their outing with you, so why don't guys do the same thing?

Example: This gentleman who on meeting the first time decided on a casual evening with a walk planned, we had such a lovely time that he asked me out on a date of fine dining. He was very successful, actually renowned, and knew how to dress for special events. When taking me out the second time for an evening of dining, he wore a ball cap, casual clothes, and running shoes; exactly what he wore on our casual outing.

I was very disappointed. By dressing in this manner, his message to me; "Neither I or the evening was significant enough to dress to impress." I didn't date him again. If you want to wear your ball cap, sneakers, jeans, bomber jacket go ahead but not on a date or an evening out with your significant other.

A WOMAN wants to date a MAN, not a guy!

I must speak on personal grooming. What's with the nose hair, the stained teeth, body smell or no scent at all? Women have to tweeze and wax their eyebrows; painful! You guys just have to clip your nose hair once a week, if that; honestly I don't see the problem. Most whiteners come with easy instructions, deodorant must be used on a daily basis at least twice a day and cologne to complete your presentation. Did you know that cologne is a female aphrodisiac?

Example: I went out on a dinner date with this guy who had the most amazing eyes, but I was continuously distracted by his nose hair. Yea guys, nose hair. His eyes would have gotten a kiss good night. Instead, it was an extended handshake and a good night salutation.

Example: Dated this man who didn't wear cologne; when asked; he expressed that women liked the natural scent of a man. That's partly true but this is how most of us women think; evening we want the arousal of his cologne scent, the morning we want the arousal of his manly scent. The first date asks if she's allergic to colognes.

Moses and Santa Claus look-a-likes, what's up with that? You do know that both these men came with some important attributes to attract the women, right? One parted water, saved people and climbed mountains; the other brings gifts, love, and joy to the world on an airborne sleigh.

I don't know if you're dreamers or hopefuls, but this I can confirm without even meeting you, their attributes you don't have. So here's the deal; keep the beard trim or shave it off, and get your hair cut and styled. I've had women say to me, "I love Santa Claus, he's magical. He brings the little girl out in me at Christmas time, but I don't want to date him."

I would like to mention jewelry; I'm personally impressed when I see a man wearing jewelry. It tells me he knows and takes complete ownership with the confidence of his style. Keep it straightforward and tasteful allowing for a five-star response.

There are many types of clothing styles for guys, but personality-wise, and generally speaking, there are four main archetypes, figure out which one or two combine is all about you:

Gallant
Urbane
Youthful
Stylish

GALLANT: The Gentleman Style. He appreciates the finer things in life, admired, and well respected by his peers, friends, and he's selective with whom he calls friends. Well versed on a variety of subjects that interest him, and communicates them with an ease of confidence and fortitude. Although he enjoys socializing, he is somewhat of a loner. An evening out would be a dinner at a quiet but significant restaurant, followed by an art exhibit or theater. In regards to women; he knows of chivalry, thought of as charming and established. The adjectives that would best describe him would be refined, cultured, gracious, and accomplished.

To describe him in a word: **POWER**

Designer suits (silk is a favorite fabric), silk ties and pocket squares that make a statement of power, tweeds are welcomed as well. Designer dress shoes and sandals are definite along with sneakers but only worn when needed. At a casual affair, you will be dressed in a turtle or round neck sweater with dress pants or jeans. Tailored top coat or raincoat with scarfs along with a hat will express your style. Tasteful designer gold jewelry speaks confidence. Conservative colors; a pastel is acceptable as an accessory.

URBANE: The Corporate Style. He appreciates success; the cup is half full type attitude and makes an effort to be not for show but gains. He has two sets of friends; ones that will assist in him achieving his goals, actually I would call them acquaintances but he refers to them as friends, the other are his real friends that he keeps very close to his heart. He enjoys conversing on subjects that relate to his success. He works hard and plays hard, that's his life quote. An evening out would be going to an event then meeting up with friends for a late dinner or drinks at one of his favorite meeting places. In regards to women, he knows that of being sensuous and thought of as suave and dynamic. The adjectives that best describe him would be adventurous, witty, confident and successful.

To describe him in a word: **DYNAMIC**

You do have business suits with noticeable accessories. Designer form fitting jeans with a sports or suit jacket is also your style. Designer casual shoes, sneakers and sandals for look and comfort accessorizing your jeans and T-shirt. Round neck sweater with dress shirt is your style. If you have a coat, it would be a raincoat with an urban look in black. Jewelry is a mixture of metals, designs, and the piece would have to have some significance in your life for you to wear it. Varied colors are acceptable if they reflect success.

YOUTHFUL: The Boy Next Store Style. He appreciates his life and the people in it. Being noticed is only important when trying to find his friends that he's arranged to meet. Family and friends are his priority, and they are what he loves most about his life. He's there for a shoulder to cry on, and well-liked by his peers, neighbours, and friends. He enjoys conversing on a variety of subjects that are his interests and hobbies. He enjoys socializing but needs time alone for his interests. He's into sports, outdoors and casual lifestyle. An evening out would be going to a sports event or concert, ending at his favorite pub with friends. In regards to women, he knows that of being amorous and thought of as thoughtful and communicative. The adjectives that best describe him would be casual, unpretentious, giving and friendly.

To describe him in a word: **GENUINE**

You wear your suit only for special occasions like date night. A casual dress shirt or t-shirt with form fitting jeans and a sports jacket is you. Ball caps and khakis are part of your wardrobe with Nike sneakers and casual sandals, with one pair of dress shoes. Designer apparel is your thing but only if you like how it looks and feels. Colors vary from white to bright; you are quite comfortable either way. Jewelry is right when it shows well.

STYLISH: The Fashion Guru Style. He appreciates going and doing, events, happenings, parties. Being noticed is his ultimate goal hence fashion is a priority in his dress. He will know all the fashion trends. His calendar, cell phone, and social media are his means of survival. He's very popular although most are pretentious and self-fulfilling, and he's very much aware of who they are. He chooses very carefully who he calls a friend and values them like a rare jewel, and they reciprocate the same. He's a communicator so you will see him networking as the major part of his conversing. An evening out would be a networking event then meeting up with friends over drinks for fun and merriment. In regards to women, he knows that of being gracious, thought of as entertaining and spontaneous. The adjectives that best describe him would be trendy, in vogue, engaging, exciting and detail thinker.

To describe him in a word: **INSPIRE**

You are Mr. Vogue! He knows the trends both in personal and business wear. You can go from vintage to ultra-modern or from dramatic to simply subtle with jewelry as well. It's a must to have a designer suit, tie and pocket square in black with designer black dress shoes. To keep with the trends; you will accessorize this black suit. You know how to relax while still making a fashion statement. You might be one type of personal style but most likely a combination.

Don't forget the Bowtie in your wardrobe!

DATING ADVICE

Law of Attraction is the charismatic influence of the Cosmos that draws similar energies together.

Love, at First Sight, is meeting someone and knowing you're in love with them the minute your eyes connect.

Generally speaking, dating is more about the law of attraction than it's about love at first sight. I believe in "love at first sight" because I'm a hopeful romantic but realistically the "law of attraction" happens to most of us. Dating is not easy sometimes it can be tormenting, but then if you find that someone special it's all worth it.

I believe you can change your whole attitude on dating if you think of it as an entrepreneur. You know like branding, marketing, and strategy of the business or product.

Branding yourself is about determining your important traits which will distinguish you from others while magnetizing the interest of that special someone you want in your life. An effective brand gives you a major edge over your competition.

Today, in the dating scene you have to know how to navigate yourself to get results. There's never been a time that has made it easy to meet another and yet so complicated or maybe impersonal.

Promoting yourself is a must and when you think about it, if it's going to help you find love, why not? I call it **'The 5 W's Dating Strategy'**: What, Why, Where, Who, and When!

Why do you want this someone in your life? The why is important, being specific brings clarity. **Example:** short term, long term, dating companion, travel partner and so on.

Who is this someone? Be specific in identifying this someone you want in your life. **Example:** personality traits, goals, interests, and so on that are imperative to you in a relationship.

What are your needs and wants in the relationship? You need to identify your wants and needs in order to have a connection of familiarity. **Example:** the glass is half full type personality; someone who the glass is half empty type personality would probably not be a good choice but again clarity of wants and needs is necessary.

Where will you meet this someone? Develop a strategy a plan on where you'd meet this someone. **Example:** online dating, meet-up groups, speed dating, singles supper clubs, and sports clubs; be creative and don't limit yourself because you could be missing a wonderful opportunity.

When should you begin? Commitment of time, effort, and enthusiasm is what's going to bring you success. **Example:** attitude plays a very important part and monetizing your time will help in achieving your goals.

By the way, you can use Strategy to provide a descriptive profile on an online dating site.

Your to-do list when on a date:

1. **PLAN** the date, and get her approval.
2. **PHONE** conversation before the first date.
3. **PREPARE** by learning about one to three of her interests for discussion purposes.
4. **MANNERS** refer to Chivalry Reigns, memorize them.
5. **DRESS** appropriately for your date plans, and be well-groomed.
6. **BE ON TIME** is a must, but if you are going to be a few minutes late, let her know.
7. **CELL PHONE** on silence, no texting or phone calls while on the date.
8. **CONFIDENCE** attracts confidence.
9. **POSITIVE ATTITUDE** no one likes misery.

10. COMPLIMENT her style, features, intelligence but no body parts. Make them flirty and sincere.

11. LENGTH of the first date should be two hours to two and a half hours, no more.

12. BODY LANGUAGE is important, so watch her actions, do your research.

13. FLIRTATIOUS energy is a good thing while being subtle.

14. QUESTIONS are good, but not in an interview form. Ask a question, pause in silence for the reply.

15. LISTEN to what she has to say, don't interrupt.

16. SMILE it's welcoming and encouraging.

17. EYE CONTACT shows you're interested.

18. CONVERSATION should be interesting and fun.

19. HONESTY is the best policy.

20. JOKES are limited and in good taste.

21. FINANCES, EX'S, GOSSIP prohibited in your conversation.

22. KISSING "Keep It Simple Sweetheart" on the first date.

23. DRINKING in moderation is accepted.

24. TOPICS in conversation should be light, fun and refreshing. Check out the trivia section or the questions of interest.

25. COLOGNE careful on how much you put on

26. SMOKING no can do until you've said good night.

27. REPEAT back what she says and follow up with a question.

28. VOICE TONE an expressive voice is pleasant to listen to along with speed and tone. Your tone should be flexible while eliminating loudness. A gentle voice that's commanding is seductive and appreciated.

29. SICK stay home, apologize and arrange another time.

30. RELAX – Real **E**qual **L**ead **A**ttentive **X**enial

Let me give you an example of one of my experiences while dating, I will refer to **#21** as an example. Met this lovely man for a drink, and then we went for dinner. Through the dinner he only spoke of his estranged wife and their divorce. What do you think my decision on a second date would have been?

Oh another thing; some guys think they've played a woman, unless you have astute listening skills along with being very observant I can tell you with no hesitation, you were the one played.

No matter how charming and sincere you present yourself, women's senses are on alert. Players are not bad guys; they're just not men! There are no winners in this game, just losers! When guys play this game, women control the destiny.

Will
Oust
Male
Ego
Nonsense

Did You Know

This section is about the trivia of love. Why trivia? Have you ever been on a date where there's a pause in the conversation? Awkward! Trivia works well to kick-start a conversation, bringing either humour or knowledge or both into play.

- Only 4% of the male population asks their girlfriend's parents' for approval, for their daughter's hand in marriage.

- The expression "tying the knot" dates to Roman times when the bride wore a girdle that was tied in knots, which the groom then had the fun of untying.
- The oldest sex manual was published in China 5000 years ago.
- 6% of men propose to their girlfriends over the phone.
- 1 out of 5 men proposes on bended knee.
- Studies show that men, who kiss their wives or girlfriends before leaving in the morning; live five years longer, earn a higher income, are more methodical and more stable than men who don't. It was believed that birds chose their mates on February 14 hence Valentine's Day.
- Because doves mate for life, they have become a symbol of fidelity.
- 2 out of 5 people marry their first love.
- The average engagement lasts six months.
- 53% of all mass-market paperback books sold in the USA are romanced novels.
- The first diamond engagement ring was presented in 1477. Recent research indicates that around 9000 romantic couples each year take out marriage licenses and fail to use them.
- The word "aphrodisiac" is derived from the Greek Goddess of romance & beauty: Aphrodite.
- In the 1950s, a woman prepared dinner for her man and made sure it was on time, and very little noise or conversation came into play – dinner was a quiet time. Now, dinner is a time to meet and socialize with family and friends; it has nothing to do with appetite or designated time. Nor is there a designated gender to prepare meals anymore.
- Nearly 25% of women pay their way on a date.
- A fairly passionate kiss burns an average of nine calories.
- 52% of men would rather their partner surprise them with a gift instead of asking them what they would like.

- The average person in their lifetime will spend an estimated 20,160 minutes kissing.
- The reason that the engagement ring and the wedding band was worn on the fourth finger of the left hand is because the ancient Egyptians thought that the "vein of love" ran from this finger directly to the heart.
- In ancient times, when couples got married they would go into seclusion. People would bring honey and place it outside their door so to keep their relationship sweet for the length of seclusion which would usually last one moon cycle, hence the "HONEYMOON"!
- It's said that Casanova ate 50 Oysters every evening. It's said that Casanova would feed oysters by mouth to his women.
- Juno, Queen of Heaven who rules over marriage, the hearth and childbirth, the month of June takes its name from her, making it the most appropriate for weddings.
- It's reported that more than 10,000 marriages a year are traceable to romances which began during coffee breaks.
- 50% of all people have their first kiss before the age of 14 years. Ancient Egyptians never kissed with their mouths; instead, they kissed with their noses.
- Our brains have special neurons that help us find each other's lips in the dark.
- In 2000, the average age of a bride was 24 years, and the average age of a groom was 28 years.
- The veil dates back to Ancient Rome, when it was flame yellow always worn over the face, and called flam meum.
- According to English folklore, Saturday, the most popular American choice for marriage, is the most unlucky day to marry.
- The experts insist that the average person falls in love seven times before marriage.

- The heart is the most common symbol of romantic love. The heart is red in color, hence why the color of love and romance is red.
- Ancient cultures believed the heart to be the source of emotion and intellect.
- The wedding cake in Roman times was made with wheat because wheat represented fertility to bear children.
- The term "spooning" was coined in Wales in the 1700's. Welsh men would send a lady that they felt affectionate towards a decorative spoon to let her know of his intentions. If she was interested, she would then wear the spoon on a ribbon around her neck or place it on display from her window.
- The tradition that a woman should stay on the man's left side was initiated back in the early days for couple reasons:
- Protect her from garbage that in the past was thrown out of windows onto the street. Keep her away from the carriages that would spray mud and water up onto the streets.
- In the wedding ceremony it is also traditional for the bride to be on the left side of the groom, so he keeps his sword arm free to defend her.
- The sweetest day started in the 1930s during the depression as a day when acts of kindness were to be shown and given to those less fortunate. Today it includes friends, neighbors and those we love. This day is celebrated on the third Saturday of October.
- The Mexican chief Montezuma considered chocolate a "love drug" and drank 50 cups of chocolate a day before visiting his harem of 600 women.
- A four-leaf clover is considered good luck, but it is also part of an Irish love ritual. In some parts of Ireland, if a woman eats a four-leaf clover while thinking about a man, supposedly he will fall in love with her.

- The Italian city of Verona, where Shakespeare's lovers Romeo and Juliet lived, receives about 1,000 letters addressed to Juliet every Valentine's Day.

If you're not all in with the trivia aspect, then try these questions of interests to start a conversation because they're fun and refreshing. I can tell you if I was on a date especially the first and he asked me one of these questions, I would be impressed. By the way, have the answers in regards to yourself, she might come back asking you the same.

1. If you had two weeks to live and money was not an issue, how would you spend your time?
2. You're given a day to spend with a famous person; who would the person be and how would you spend that day?
3. What period in history would you have wanted to live? Why?
4. What country would you choose to lead?
5. What famous quote has influenced your life?
6. If you were a song, what's its title?
7. How would your friends describe you?
8. How would you define love?
9. What is your favourite cuisine? Why?
10. What is your most appreciated life lesson?
11. What would be your dream life?
12. If you were a book, what would be the title?
13. Describe your uniqueness using five adjectives?
14. What would you consider a "perfect" day to be?
15. What are three character traits you search for in others?
16. If you were fabric what would it be?
17. Describe a romantic moment

THE "MR" FACTOR

A guy is momentary; a man is forever. When a guy achieves the "**MR**" Factor, he transforms into a man, and that's what women want. The "**MR**" Factor will leave her powerless, and in awe of you, I know this because women have told me over, and over again they want a man, not a guy (boy). I too have experienced the difference, and it's entrancing to be with an "**MR**."

By the way, this has nothing to do with your monetary value. I have met rich guys who are not men! Look, money can't make you a man no matter how much you think it does. Women want a man who's successful and financially secure; it makes women know he has a direction and goals he wishes to achieve which gives her a sense of security!

But if you think that's what it's all about, enjoy several relationships and possibly a miserable marriage, should you get married. The men I have known who live the "**MR**" Factor personify a power that women can't resist. What is the "**MR**" Factor? He is a Man of Romance. A gentleman who has the following eight principles:

Sensuality – five senses
Exclusive – connoisseur
Lionhearted – chivalry
Fashionable – style
Honest – communication
Entertaining – fun
Loving – romance
Power - confidence

These eight principles have to become a lifestyle to cultivate a lasting and loving relationship. The Man of Romance understands the power of a thank you for her love thus leaving her powerless to resist the very thought of him.

I've heard guys say; "Love is complicated, I have obligations like job expectations, life priorities and she doesn't get it!" Believe me when I say, "She gets it!" She just wants you to get it; she has to know you're thankful for her love. When a man is an "MR", he never hesitates to thank the woman he loves for her love, and in response, she will do the same.

Here's a suggestion: While developing the "MR" Factor take at least 10% of your week, and make it about romance.

Whether it's calling her in the middle of the day to say I love you, sending her flowers when she's having a tough day, planning a date night or being her shoulder to cry on, doing that something meaningful and unexpected. Her appreciation will be gratifying.

I can't say this enough; romance is the thank you in love! The eight principles of the "MR" Factor are throughout the book; learn, and live them.

"Your smile warms my heart,
Your laughter ignites my soul."

Colleen C. Carson

ROMANTIC
C⚥NNECTION

"WHEN I HOLD THE HAND OF THE MAN I LOVE;
I FEEL THE NAKEDNESS OF OUR FLESH IN TOUCH,
FINGERS ENTWINED SANCTIONING US IN
THOUGHT, AND THE GRAVITY OF OUR HOLD
EMPOWERING THE GENTLE PULSE OF OUR HEARTS
ALIVE IN EACH OTHER...WITH A GENTLE SQUEEZE
OUR SOULS BECOME ONE."

LANGUAGE

OF

LOVE

Short Poetry Version:

Your touch like a feather in a spring breeze
Our sensual kisses in the desire of we
My body captive in your caress
I breathe a whisper of a loving yes

OR

Long Poetry Version

Your touch like a feather in a spring breeze
Our sensual kisses in the desire of we
My body captive in your caress
I breathe a whisper of a loving yes

A desiring thirst of each a start
Your longing gaze devours my heart
Awaken passion of rhapsody
Our oneness sighs in fantasy

My heart pulses in joyful bliss
Cherish by your butterfly kiss
Embraced in tranquil serenity
Our love forever a melody

Colleen C. Carson

For centuries poems and prose have been written about the love of one to another. I don't believe you have to be a poet or a writer to achieve this intention.

Many of us would adore the experience of receiving a poem or prose from the one we love. Don't get caught up in the rhyming, and lose thought of your true feelings, if you're finding it difficult than just a picture with a powerful word of expression can be just as significant.

Proses have a natural flow of speech rather than a regular structure as in traditional poetry, and it doesn't have to be several verses, it can be as short as one verse. Whichever you choose, allow your heart to express your true feelings while using the Language of Love, it's not as complicated as you think.

Accomplished	Adorable	Adoring
Admiration	Affectionate	Amazing
Applaud	Angelic	Astonishing
Astounding	Attractive	Beautiful
Beguiling	Blissful	Breathtaking
Captivating	Caress	Caring
Charismatic	Charming	Cheerful
Cherish	Class/y	Clever
Compassionate	Compelling	Considerate
Cozy	Creative	Creation
Cuddle/y	Cute	Darling
Dazzling	Dear	Dearest
Delectable	Delicious	Desirable
Desire	Devoted	Devouring
Divine	Dreamy	Dynamic
Elegant	Embracing	Enchanting
Endearing	Engaging	Enjoyable
Enticing	Enthralling	Entrancing
Essence	Exceptional	Exquisite
Eye-catching	Fragrant	Fantasy
Fascinating	Fashionable	Feminine
Fine	Generous	Gentle
Genuine	Giving	Glamorous
Glowing	Gorgeous	Graceful

Gracious
Head over heels
Heart-felt
Hot
Illusive
Incredible
Inspirational
Intelligent
Intimacy
Joyful
Kindly
Kissable
Loving
Luscious
Magical
Massage
Mesmerizing
Mythical
Naughty
Omniscient
Only
Passionate
Perfection
Pleasurable
Precious
Pulsating
Radiant
Ravishing
Remarkable
Romantic
Seductive
Sexual
Sinuous
Sparkling
Spicy
Stunning
Sweetheart
Tasteful
Tenderness
Tranquil
Ultimate

Happy
Heart
Honest
Hugs
Imaginative
Inner beauty
Inspire
Interesting
Intimate
Joyous
Kind-hearted
Lovable
Loyal
Luxurious
Magnetic
Memorable
Motivating
Naked
Nestled
Oneness
Panache
Peaceful
Playful
Poetic
Pretty
Pure
Rapture
Red-hot
Riveting
Rose
Sensual
Sexy
Smart
Spellbinding
Spirited
Stylish
Sugar
Temptress
Throbbing
Treasured
Understanding

Haunting
Heavenly
Honey
Huggable
Impressive
Innocent
Inspiring
Intriguing
Inviting
Juicy
Kiss
Love
Lustful
Magic
Majestic
Memory
Mysterious
Natural
Very Nice
Opulent
Passion
Piquant
Pleasing
Powerful
Princess
Quivering
Rapturous
Relaxing
Romance
Satisfying
Sensuous
Sincere
Softly
Special
Striking
Sweet
Talented
Tender
Touching
Truly
Unique

Unforgettable	Unusual	Valentine
Vibrant	Victorious	Vigorous
Virtuous	Vision	Vital
Vivacious	Vixen	Warming
Welcoming	Whimsical	Wicked
Wild	Willowy	Wistful
Womanly	Yours	Youthful
Yearning	Yummy	Zealous

The Language of Love is meant to assist you in learning how to use words to give compliments as well; there are much more if you wish to research. A compliment should reflect appreciation and desire for your significant other.

Example: You're taking her out, and she will spend hours getting ready. She will expect a compliment from you for the time and thought she has devoted in dressing for you.

Poor compliment: "You look nice."

Desire compliment: "Wow, you're captivating!"

The latter indicates that you notice and appreciate her; the other sounds like an obligation to acknowledge. Voice tone along with visual response is imperative. Remember a gentle voice that's commanding is seductive.

Giving a compliment on how she is dressed:

- View her from her feet to her eyes
- Gaze into her eyes
- Sigh
- Pause
- With a gentle, sexy tone
- Express the compliment

- Gaze into her eyes
- Sigh
- Pause
- With a gentle, sexy tone
- Lean into her
- Whisper the compliment in her ear

Another approach:

- Take a moment
- Look at her with gratitude
- Express personal admiration

Remember the "KISS" approach

We all want compliments, but it must be personal to be appreciated. Women are frustrated with hearing the lack of originality when given a compliment. It's important when giving a compliment; it's genuine, respectful, and original, but also about her with an added touch of sexy enthusiasm. She'll know when it isn't sincere. A compliment is to praise or express admiration for someone.

Kindly

Imaginative

Sincere

Sensuous

FLOWER SENSE

There has been a symbolic meaning for flowers since Adam and Eve. In past eras, when public expressions of love and affection were forbidden, lovers exchanged roses to translate their feelings of love.

The giving of a bouquet of red roses can be rather generic, why not personalize the bouquet and make it about her. Give time and thought when giving flowers to anyone in your life but particularly to that special someone.

Example: A dozen roses in assorted colors and each rose tagged with a personality trait about her:

Red-loving, yellow-friend, peach-sincerity, blue-extraordinary, white-humility, coral-desirable and so on, do you see where I'm going with this?

Duplicate colours if need be using a different trait, she will be in awe at your thoughtfulness.

Example: An assortment of flowers:

Orchid-elegant, Iris-wisdom, Daffodil-kind, Sunflower-adoring, Ivy-affectionate, Tulip-passionate, Calla Lily-beauty

On your floral card you write; "Twelve reasons what I love about you."

The Rose: symbolizes an immortal love that will live forever even after death – month of June

- Rosebuds - a new love

- Red Rose - love and passion

- White Rose - innocence and humility

- Crème Rose – charm and thoughtfulness
- Pink Rose - romance and femininity
- Deeper pink Rose - gratitude, and admiration
- Orange Rose - fascination and eagerness
- Peach Rose - sincerity and sensitivity
- Blue Rose - enchanting and extraordinary
- Lilac Rose - magnetism and charm
- Green Rose - growth and encouragement
- Yellow Rose - friendship and optimism
- Coral Rose - desire and attraction
- Salmon Rose – enthusiasm and excitement

The volume of Roses:

Single rose – symbolizes "Thank you."

Two roses – symbolizes "I love us."

Six roses – symbolizes "I desire you."

Ten roses – symbolizes "Forever always."

Twelve roses – symbolizes "Be mine."

Thirteen roses – symbolizes "I'm your secret admirer."

Fifteen roses – symbolizes "I'm sorry."

The Carnation: symbolizes love's fascination and affection – month of January

- White - pure love
- Red - passionate love
- Pink - tender love
- Yellow – friendship

The Daisy: innocence and purity – month of April

The Hyacinths: symbolizes game, play, and sport

- White - love

- Yellow - friendship

- Purple - forgiveness

- Blue - loyalty

The Iris: symbolizes nobility, valour, and faith

The Orchid: symbolizes refinement, elegance, seduction, and preciousness

The Pansy: symbolizes you're in my thoughts always

The Peony: symbolizes success and prosperity

The Violet: symbolizes modesty, quiet love, humility, faithfulness, and virtue – month of February

The Aster: symbolizes charm and patience – month of September

The Chrysanthemum: symbolizes innocence, cheerfulness, and loyal love – month of November

The Dahlia: symbolizes dignity and elegance

The Iris: symbolizes faith, hope, and wisdom

The Lily: symbolizes purity and faith

The Peruvian Lily: symbolizes friendship and devotion

The Calla Lily: symbolizes sophistication and beauty

The Snapdragon: symbolizes desire and strength

The Tulip: symbolizes a perfect lover and passion

The Sunflower: symbolizes adoration and sunshine

The Morning Glory: symbolizes love, affection or mortality – month of September

The Gardenia: symbolizes purity, joy, and secret love

The Lily of the Valley: symbolizes happiness, sweetness, and completeness –month of May

The Daffodil: symbolizes regard for others - month is March

The Freesia: symbolizes innocence

The Stephanotis: symbolizes marital happiness

The Forget-Me-Not: symbolizes true love and memories

The Magnolia: symbolizes love of nature, nobility, and perseverance

The Hydrangea: symbolizes understanding

The Baby's Breath: symbolizes innocence

The Gladiolus: symbolizes strength and moral integrity – month of August

The Fuchsia: symbolizes amiability

The Marigold: symbolizes sacred affection – month of October

The Tiger Lily: symbolizes wealth and pride

The Hibiscus: symbolizes delicate beauty

The Water Lily: symbolizes antiquity and enlightenment – month of July

The Poinsettia: symbolizes good cheer, success, and celebration – month of December

BEDAZZLE HER

When selecting jewelry, give it as much thought, in the same way as with flower sense.

GOLD: relates to the Sun, happiness, spiritual love, quests of the heart

SILVER: relates to the Moon, feminine energy, romance, purity, trust

BIRTHSTONE GEMS

- **January** - Garnet
- **February** - Amethyst
- **March** - Aquamarine or Bloodstone
- **April** - Diamond
- **May** - Emerald
- **June** - Moonstone or Pearl
- **July** - Carnelian or Ruby
- **August** - Peridot or Sardonyx
- **September** - Sapphire
- **October** - Opal or Tourmaline
- **November** - Topaz
- **December** - Lapis Lazuli or Turquoise

BIRTHSTONES

- **Garnet:** believed to endow with cheerfulness, strength, and sincerity
- **Amethyst:** believed to bestow the powers to stimulate, and soothe both the mind and emotions
- **Aquamarine:** believed to bestow continuous happiness and love
- **Bloodstone:** believed to bestow courage, wisdom, and vitality
- **Carnelian:** believed to diffuse unpleasant thoughts and sorrow
- **Diamond:** believed to enhance inner self, creativity, and originality
- **Emerald:** believed to bestow an accommodating and pleasant disposition
- **Garnet:** believed to enhance sensuality, sexuality, and regeneration
- **Lapis Lazuli:** believed to bring happiness, love, and prosperity
- **Moonstone:** believed to bring good luck, reflection, and fertility
- **Opal:** believed to bestow pure thoughts, faithfulness, and inspiration
- **Pearl:** believed to enhance integrity, focus, and protection
- **Peridot:** believed to enhance loyalty, friendship, and happiness
- **Ruby:** believed to protect against false friendships and warn of imminent danger
- **Sapphire:** believed to bring comfort, courage, and strength
- **Sardonyx:** believed to endow with honesty, mercy, and willpower

- **Topaz:** believed to bring its wearer recognition, wealth, and protection from evil
- **Tourmaline:** believed to bring happiness, generosity, and prosperity
- **Turquoise:** believed to be a pledge of friendship when given as a gift, good health, and success

GEMSTONES

- **Agate:** believed to endow calmness, longevity, and wealth
- **Cat's Eye:** believed to warn its owner of approaching danger and long life
- **Coral:** believed an amulet against natural disasters, disease, and jealous friends
- **Crystal:** believed in having healing powers, purity, and simplicity
- **Jade:** believed to endow harmonious living, justice, and modesty
- **Onyx:** believed to bring its wearer marital bliss, clearness, and dignity
- **Zircon:** believed a charm against jealousy and theft
- **Emerald:** believed to bestow an accommodating and pleasant disposition
- **Garnet:** believed to enhance sensuality, sexuality, and regeneration
- **Lapis Lazuli:** believed to bring happiness, love, and prosperity
- **Moonstone:** believed to bring good luck, reflection, and fertility
- **Opal:** believed to bestow pure thoughts, faithfulness, and inspiration
- **Pearl:** believed to enhance integrity, focus, and protection

- **Peridot:** believed to enhance loyalty, friendship, and happiness
- **Ruby:** believed to protect against false friendships and warn of imminent danger
- **Sapphire:** believed to bring comfort, courage, and strength
- **Sardonyx:** believed to endow with honesty, mercy, and willpower
- **Topaz:** believed to bring its wearer recognition, wealth, and protection from evil
- **Tourmaline:** believed to bring happiness, generosity, and prosperity
- **Turquoise:** believed to be a pledge of friendship, good health, and success

ROMANTIC ACCENTS

Creating a romantic ambiance is styled with such details to create the sensuality of romance. Here are some suggestions:

Rose Petals
Soft or Tinted Lighting
Array of Flowers
Champagne Glasses
Sexy Blindfold
Pillows
Faux Rug
Lingerie/Robes
Sex Toys
Lace
Love Letter
Element of Surprise
Massage Lotions/Oils
Bubble Bath
Personal Gifts
Satin/Silk Linen

Candles
Sexy Card Game
Mood Music
Champagne
Feathers
Soft Blankets
Fireplace
Red Accessories
Picnic Basket
Lavender Scent
Sexy Invite
Chocolates
Mirrors
Perfume/Cologne
Romantic Poetry
Sensual Literature

ROMANTIC GIFTS

Bouquet   of   Flowers

Here are a few romantic suggestions on gift-giving (remember to refer to The Mystery of She section):

- Jewelry
- Perfume
- An Evening of Dancing
- A Rose
- Chocolates preferably Truffles
- Her Favourite Candy
- Basket of Bath/Beauty items
- Basket of Fresh Fruit
- Beautiful Journal
- Silk/Satin Bath Robe
- Lingerie
- A Spa Day
- Shopping Day
- Pedicure
- Manicure
- Romantic Dinner
- Dinner Cruise
- Theater/Concert Tickets
- Candle Set
- Heart Shaped Dish
- Weekend Getaway
- Sensual Bedroom

- Bottle of Champagne
- Crystal Flutes
- Handbag
- Framed Picture of You Both
- Footwear
- Wine Tour with her Girlfriends
- Heart Shaped Balloons
- A Good Read
- Beautiful Scarf/Shawl
- Limousine Service
- Massage
- Catered Picnic
- A Romantic Letter or Poem
- Night at a Hotel

Gift giving is part of the romance in your relationship except for the first month of a new relationship, again through personal choice. I have had several men and women come to me and ask, "What do I do when I meet a person just before their birthday, Christmas or Valentine's Day?" The question is, "What do you want to do?"

My suggestion is that if it's within the first month of your meeting a salutation with a simple gift is sufficient; a card, a flower, or a bottle of wine. Certainly, a greeting in the first week is enough, and nothing more.

Gift giving has always been about personal choice. How seriously do you feel about this person and how do they feel about you? Time is not the factor; it's about your feelings for each other; you can't put a price tag on love.

TOP 30 AUTHOR'S SONG PICKS

What would we do without love songs? Romantic dining would just be a dinner; the glass of wine by the fireplace would not be as enjoyable. Music is the core of creating a sensuous ambiance and memory. I know we all have stories to tell of songs leaving a personal memory. During a romantic moment do not hesitate to dance together; a memory you both won't forget!

You Don't Touch Me Like You Do	DocJ - Guyed Bk
Hello	Lionel Ritchie
The Way You Look Tonight	Harry Connick Jr.
Adore You	Miley Cyrus
Rest Of My Life	Bruno Mars
'Til The End Of Time	Timothy Bloom
Endless Love	Luther Vandross
Like I'm Gonna Lose You	Meghan Trainor
Thinking Out Loud	Ed Sheeran
I'll Make Love To You	BoyzIIMen
Unforgettable	Nat King Cole
I Want To Grow Old With You	Westlife
Secret	Seal
Close Your Eyes	Michael Buble
Let's Make Love	Hill/McGraw
All Of Me	John Legend
Come Away With Me	Norah Jones
Chasing Cars	Snow Patrol
Back At One	Brian McKnight
You Sang To Me	Mark Anthony
Besame Mucho	Diana Krall
Love Someone	Jason Mraz
My Valentine	Martina McBride
Take Me To Your Heart	Michael Learns
Breathless	Shayne Ward
Right Here Waiting	Richard Marx
This I Promise You	Nsync
Would You Still Love Me Brian	Nhira
A Thousand Years	Christina Perri
La Vie En Rose	Dean Martin

101 MAGICAL MOMENTS

1. Romantic kisses; the back of their hand, forehead, cheek, shoulder, and head.
2. While holding hands, every so often squeeze it their hand gently.
3. Take a walk in the rain.
4. Cuddle on the beach with hot chocolate during the winter season and watch the snow fall.
5. Build a snowman together.
6. Go skinny dipping.
7. Send sexy texts to each other.
8. Feed each other food with your fingers.
9. Build a sandcastle together.
10. Find your private beach and sunbathe nude.
11. During a conversation, lean over and kiss your partner gently on the cheek or forehead.
12. Order a heart-shaped cake or pizza with your names on it and feed each other.
13. Go to an ice cream parlour and share.
14. Go horseback riding and stop for a picnic.
15. Cloud is watching; describe what each other sees.
16. Go back to the place you first met and share your thoughts of that first encounter.
17. Re-create your first date.

18. Go ice-skating or rollerblading together.
19. Make love in a field.
20. Build a tent surrounded by candles in front of your fireplace with mood music.
21. Cuddle in bed and listen to the morning rain.
22. Stay in bed the entire day.
23. Have a song dedicated to them on the radio.
24. Sleep together under the stars cuddling.
25. Cook your lover they're favourite meal.
26. Have a finger food picnic by candlelight on the beach while watching the sunset.
27. Together you select an "Our Song."
28. Create a 'YouTube' video about your love.
29. Buy a bar of soap and carve in it: "You've cleansed my Heart."
30. Romanize your bedroom for an intimate evening.
31. Give a teddy bear with a love message.
32. Wash each other's hair.
33. In the morning, get your partner's toothbrush ready by putting toothpaste on it.
34. Make dinner together in just aprons.
35. On a full moon, evening soaks in a hot tub nude together surrounded by candles.
36. Dance in each other's arms in the kitchen while cooking dinner.
37. Cuddle up and roast marshmallows on the barbecue.
38. The evening of their birthday, wrap yourself up in a big red bow and sing her "Happy Birthday."
39. Dance under the stars on a warm, breezy summer night.
40. Go boating to an island where you have a romantic dinner planned.
41. Tell your lover when least expected that you love them.
42. Go for a walk while it's snowing.

43. Go on a hayride in the moonlight night.
44. A mannerly attitude is romantic.
45. Go to the park and push each other on a swing.
46. Go to an amusement park with a child's reaction.
47. Make love in different areas of your home.
48. While on a walk, pick a flower and place it in their hair.
49. Have a shower and wash each other slowly.
50. Have a luxurious bubble bath by candlelight.
51. Draw a heart with both your initials in the sand.
52. Make your lover lunch to take to work with a note inside describing in detail how you are sexually going to satisfy them that evening.
53. Walk along the shore of a lake or the ocean at sunset.
54. Have a code for your sexual parts, and refer to that code during a night out with friends, only both of you will know what you're saying to each other; VERY SEXY.
55. Drive to a romantic setting and make love.
56. Write your lover a poem or song.
57. Read an erotic story while cuddling.
58. When dining; order a platter for two and eat from the platter while feeding each other.
59. Go on a sleigh ride.
60. Camp out in your backyard under the stars.
61. Tell your lover how much to love them on a billboard where they'll see on the way to work.
62. Take dancing lessons together.
63. Dedicate a star in their name and show them.
64. Bring your lover coffee/tea in the morning.
65. Cook a heart-shaped food breakfast.
66. Go to a karaoke bar and surprise your lover by getting up and singing "your song" to them.
67. Leave morning love notes around the house.
68. Stay at a hotel for a weekend.

69. Ride a bicycle built for two through a park.
70. Walk and play in the fallen leaves in autumn.
71. Dress in costume and role-play.
72. Give your lover a kiss when they least expect it.
73. Go on a mystery weekend cruise.
74. Wake your lover up by making love to them.
75. Order a milkshake with two straws.
76. Take an early morning walk to watch the sunrise.
77. Fly a kite on a breezy day.
78. Make something out of pottery or wood.
79. Go on a horse-drawn carriage ride.
80. Leave a note at the entry of your home saying, "Follow my heart trail; your destiny is that of intimate passion!" Strew a trail of rose petals to the bedroom where your lover will find you nude lying on the bed. Have several lit candles, sensual music, and champagne chilling to serve.
81. Park one evening in a beautiful setting, turn on a romantic song and ask your lover to dance.
82. Take a walk along a lake in the moonlight.
83. Kiss to the rhythm of music; for at least three to four songs; no sexual touching.
84. Go for a walk in silence, only touch to express your feelings.
85. Plan an intimate evening together.
86. Dance with your lover on a city street in the rain.
87. Share a piggy back ride.
88. Stare into each other's eyes for at least three minutes, and then talk about how you felt.
89. Mail your lover a handwritten love letter.
90. Go shopping together for sex toys.
91. A spontaneous drive to nowhere.
92. When standing on the escalator below, give a gentle kiss at the back of their neck.
93. While lying in bed; glide your fingertips slowly and gently outlining her body, at least three times. Do

not touch any sexual parts. Remember this is sensual, not sexual.

94. Paint each other with flavoured body paint then lick it off each other.
95. Undress each other slowly while looking at each other.
96. Dress formally for a romantic dinner at home.
97. Think of an affectionate pet name, and I don't mean honey, sweetie, or babe. Nicknames like Sunshine, Princess, Lady (her name), Magic, Beautiful, Darling, Peaches, Angel, Precious and so on. Make the pet name about her personality. By the way ladies men like pet names as well.
98. Read to your lover during their bathing.
99. Have a pillow fight.
100. Do a puzzle together by candlelight.
101. Fill your bedroom with helium balloons attaching romantic moments you have shared or romantic ideas you wish to share.

I have given you 101 suggestions for romantic moments, and there are much more... Just use your imagination. These moments offer a variety of emotions from thoughtful, loving, sensual and intimate while creating romance.

Treat each romantic moment with passion, and sensuality. Keep your conversations lighthearted and fun, don't get caught up in talking about work, children, finances, personal or relationship problems. Make it about loving each other.

PLANNED
EVENTS

"THAT SOMEDAY CAME
A DREAM GIFTED BY A SPECIAL SOMEONE
PLANNED IN ANTICIPATION OF MY JOY
BESTOWED WITH A SINGLE THREAD OF LOVE."

GARDEN OF LOVE

What You Will Need:

Choice of Flowers
Choice of Herbs
One or more Garden Tree(s)
Garden Rocks
Garden Characters
Garden Candles and Torches
Garden Sign
Fertilizer
Soil
Garden Tools
Water

Remember to refer to "The Meaning of Flowers" Section; it will help you get some ideas on what to select for the garden. First, you should choose the flowers that are best suited to her personality or taste. For instance, if her favourite colors are orange, red, pink and purple, those are the colours you choose. Next, her personality should be a reflection of the flowers you choose; if she likes pansies than include pansies. Refer to The Mystery of She section for her favourite flowers.

Herbs are a great addition to the Garden. Herbs are used for salads, cooking, and health. If your special someone loves cooking, then they'll appreciate herbs! Parsley, dill, sage, basil, thyme, and mint are some of the most popular in the herb family.

If planting a miniature tree, a Japanese willow would be a lovely choice. Place the tree in the center towards the back of the garden, for balance and effect. Rock gardens are also a good choice, especially when paired with moss.

The rocks should be no smaller than four inches in circumference and vary in size. You can paint the rocks white or leave them natural, that is your choice. Here's an idea, on each rock write a personality trait, thought, or an adjective that best describes her or him. If you need help with descriptive words, just reference the Language of Love section.

Place the rocks around the garden along with garden lighting and candles; in the evening your partner's garden will flicker with light and be noticed by all. Place a garden sign in the garden that reads: "Garden of Love."

CAR WASH

Surprise your partner one morning, and wash their car before they go out.

What you're going to need:

Bucket of Soapy Water
Hose
4 or 5 Dry Clothes
Car Polish
Vacuum
Window Cleaner
Paper Towels
Romantic Note Paper
Small Envelope
Tape

- Get up early
- Wash & Polish her car
- Vacuum inside
- Wipe down the interior
- Clean the windows inside and out
- Write a love note on the stationary paper
- Put the note in the envelope
- Tape it to the steering wheel

Love note ideas:

- Thinking about you
- I love you
- Thank you for being you
- You're my special someone
- Forever
- Have a beautiful day
- You're my happiness
- Magic is your second name

THE CALENDAR

1 Large Calendar
12 Planned Events
1 Package of Wrapping Paper
1 Big Bow
1 Card

Organizational skills and time management are imperative to be successful. You can purchase most of the above items in any gift store; the rest is about your imagination. Whether you give this as a birthday, an anniversary, a Christmas or an "I Love You" gift does not matter, what does matter is that you arrange an event each month for her. The event would be for her or both of you that is up to you!

Here is a list of suggested Events:

- A Sports' Day
- A Dinner at your Favourite Restaurant
- A Spa Day
- A Romantic Weekend Cruise
- A Dance Class
- A Pedicure & Manicure
- A Shopping Spree
- A Cleaning Service
- A Luncheon with Girlfriends
- An All Day Limousine Service
- A Fitness Day
- A Weekend Retreat
- A Romantic Picnic at Sunset
- A Breakfast in the Park at Sunrise
- A Romantic Dinner for Two (prepared by you)
- A Weekend Skiing Trip
- A Concert
- A Theatrical Play
- A Day in Bed (where you cater to her every whim)
- A Babysitter for 24 Hours
- An Intimate Bistro for Lunch Together
- An Overnight Hotel Stay

I am sure you've got some of your ideas, go ahead and try them out. You could also do this idea based on one month with an event planned each week for four weeks. Before putting these arranged events on her calendar, confirm them. Once the events are confirmed, write the event on the calendar day for each month. For instance, you plan a Golf Day for her on June 2, write on the calendar as; "Golf Day" with time, location and itinerary. Once completed, wrap the calendar with bow and card.

DATE NIGHT

A Bouquet of Flowers
A Bottle of Champagne
Restaurant Booked
Babysitter Confirmed

Follow these
instructions:

You must have the
babysitter booked
before planning the
date night. Have the
babysitter arrive at 8:00 PM, and make sure you don't
have to pick her up. About a week before, telephone your
significant other either while she is at work or home;
phone her.

- "I would like to ask you out on a date if you're not
  too busy Saturday night, let's say dinner?"
- Wait for her yes response then say;
- "Would 7:30 PM be good for you?"
- Once she confirms a yes, then you begin to plan.
- Make a reservation at her favourite restaurant.
- It must have a romantic ambiance
- Reservation for 8:30 PM
- Order her favorite flowers that you can pick up
  between 6:30-7:00 PM

On date night, you dress early and leave the house around
6:30 PM, let her know you will be back. Go

pick up the flowers and the bottle of champagne. When
arriving back home, knock on the door and wait for her to
open the door. When she opens the door, announce

yourself and wait until she invites you in (even if you live there this is called role-playing).

- Give her the flowers
- A gentle kiss on her cheek
- A beautiful compliment on how she looks
- Tell her you brought the champagne to have a drink before leaving for dinner.

The suggestions on dating;

- Refer to Chivalry Rules
- Refer to Dating Page
- Refer to Language of Love

After dinner, ask her if there is something or somewhere she would like to do before being taken home. Give suggestions; dancing, a walk, a night cap, and wait for a response.

CHRISTMAS IN JULY

A miniature potted Evergreen Tree
A string of 25 Indoor colour or clear
Mini-lights
8 Red Miniature Bows for the Tree
10 Bows for the Gifts
1 Roll of Green Ribbon
Christmas or assorted colours metallic
wrapping paper
8 Candles
Christmas Music
10 Gifts (refer to gift list)
Bottle of Champagne with two glasses

A Christmas just for your special someone, it's also about expressing to them what they mean to you. For most it's not how much it costs, it's about the effort and thought you put into making them feel special.

Here are suggestions for gifts:

GIFT LIST	NOTATION
Candy/Chocolate	You are very sweet Mini
Teddy Bear	Let's cuddle
World Map	You are my world
Compass	You lead me in the right direction
Heart-Shaped Item	You have my heart
Sparkle/s	You are the sparkle in my life
Clock/Watch	You make time mean something
Toy Car	You drive me crazy with desire
List of 7 Wonders	You are the eighth
Family Portrait	Thank you
Toy House	You make a house a home
Picture of Her	You're a picture of perfection
Star-shaped Item	You are my wish come true
Sunglasses	You are my sun
Candle	You are my flame of warmth
Dictionary	Your words have such meaning
Key	You're the key to my heart
Measuring Tape	I can't measure how much I love you
Mirror	You reflect everything I want & need in my life

Glue Stick	You are the glue that holds us together
Pen	We are the love story that has yet to be written
Pillow	I love our pillow talk
Hershey Kisses	Your kisses melt into my lips
Perfume/Cologne	The scent of you is unforgettably teasing
Memory Journal	You are what memories are all about
Rock	You are the rock in our relationship
Light Bulb	You light up my life
Spices	You spice up my life
Lace Panties	You're sexy
Hot Sauce	You're hot & sexy
Unicorn symbol	You're magical

I know you can think of more gift ideas, write them down but remember each gift has to have a notation.

Where to go shopping:

• Miniature potted evergreen trees are purchased at a nursery
• String of mini-lights can be in your Christmas decorations or at a lighting store
• Mini bows, spool of ribbon and wrapping paper in any gift shop
• You will have to shop around for the gifts, try dollar stores.
How to decorate the tree:
• Wrap the mini-lights around the tree
• Arrange and stick the bows on different branches
• Take the spool of ribbon and wrap it around the tree like a garland

Plan this on a weekend night, when you know she will have to go out in the late afternoon. Maybe arrange to have a friend of hers invite her out for a late lunch to get her out of the house. If you have children, send them to grandma's or have them stay overnight at a friend's place.

Make sure you know what time she will be arriving home, and be ready with Christmas lights on, fireplace, music playing, lit candles placed around the room, and the champagne chilled. Merry Christmas!

QUEEN FOR A DAY

Thank You Card
Limousine Service
Bottle of Champagne
Pair of Champagne Glasses
Spa Day Appointment
Makeup Appointment
New Trendy Outfit
Dinner Reservation for Two
Romantic Hotel Room
His & Her Overnight Bags
Long-stem Roses
Bag of Rose Petals (or the petals from 6 roses)
Favourite Romantic Music
Bubble Bath
Scented Votive Candles
A Lighter or Matches
A Confirmed Babysitter (if you have children)
Setting a date for this Event

Try to choose a Spa and Salon inclusive. They are listed under their service in the yellow pages. The roses and rose petals can be bought at the florist or in-store florist at your local grocery store, the liquor at the liquor store, and the other items can be purchased at a variety of department stores.

When you have set the date, book the spa day which includes:

- Hair
- Makeup
- Body Massage
- Pedicure/Manicure
- Facial

Let the Spa know of your plans for that day and evening this is imperative for the pickup time. Make them aware that there is a limousine picking her up. Once you have completed the arrangements with the spa, you can then book the limousine service. Two important steps you must take when booking a limousine service: get references, and the other is never pay in full at the time of booking.

Inform the limousine service know the date, time and address of your pick up and drop off: home, spa, restaurant, hotel and anywhere else you may be going that evening.

You should leave a lapse of a half-hour from the time of pick up at the spa to drop off at the restaurant. I suggest this: take her for a scenic drive, have some champagne, listen to her choice of music and communicate.

Let the limousine service know that you will be bringing a bottle of champagne and music of choice, request champagne glasses be chilled. Confirm with them that they have a working CD player in the limousine! Email the limousine service a schedule of events for the evening:

- 6:00   Pick me up
- 6:30   Pick her up at Spa
- 6:30   Scenic Drive
- 7:00   Arrival at restaurant
- 9:00   Drive to hotel

Your dinner reservations should be at a very romantic restaurant that she favours.

Arrange with the restaurant manager that you wish to reserve the most romantic table in the house and have a rose place at her ladies place setting before your arrival.

Next is the hotel room! A hotel close to where you will be dining is a good suggestion. Have a walk after dinner is very romantic then have your limousine service follow you until you have finished your walk.

When booking your hotel room make the hotel staff aware that you will have things to place in your room before arrival, request the earliest availability of occupancy and make sure you receive a confirmation number. Confirm your room the day before the Queen for a Day event. The day of the event, arrive at the hotel at the time of occupancy; while in your room you should do the following:

- Fold the corner of the blankets down
- Place rose on her pillow
- Sprinkle rose petals on and around the bed

Just one more thing; I know many have experienced heartbreak but don't revert to negative baggage as a resolve. There will be another as there was for me.

As I was strolling down life's path
Venturing into my world of journeys
A reflection emerged unexpectedly
Did it descend from that of a single

Scent that flows in the spring breeze
Maybe a vision of a lingering sunset
Or reminiscence of echoed words
That awoke my memory of a past love

Of how our passion wove in desire
Hearts riveted by inspired love
Words decanted in spoken thought
Our bodies electrified by a gentle touch

The beauty of joyful moments
Our majestic stance saluted by others
As we dance embraced in each other's arms
Thoughts of our destiny forever as us

Yet, gradually discerned anxiety adjoined
The unexpected of what came to be
A confuse that erupted into infinity
While our love whispered the end is nearing

My wounded heart bled of sorrow
Mourning ruled my lonely tears
Days of reflection haunted by "if only"
Sleepless nights of muted discourse

Time accomplished my heart to mend
Awakening to endorsed resolve
Diversity aspired by will of thought
Once again happiness reign over sadness

As I stand in wonder of this reflection
A smile appears with a single reason
His love is that of a memory
For I share my love in another's heart

A FARE
CHANCE

"THIS IS ONLY THE BEGINNING HE RECITED WHILE FEEDING ME IN
DELIGHTFUL BITES SIPPING ON OUR WINE OF CHOICE
IN AMBIANCE OF ANTICIPATION."

CULINARY SENSUALITY

Most sensuous foods are cold in temperature, creamy in texture and high in zinc. Food does play a huge part in romance; not only by setting the mood but also by making the sexual act more erotic and satisfying.

Food and sex have been acknowledging their partnership since as far back as Adam and Eve and the forbidden fruit! Food can be very sensual and set up a romantic ambiance. For instance;

Cleopatra fed grapes to her lovers while lounging, and the great Casanova fed oysters to his women while they bathed. Radishes were considered a seductive food in Ancient Egypt while sweet potatoes in the Elizabethan Era. Ginseng, chili peppers, and garlic are notorious stimulants and have been for many eras. Since time immemorial, food is to sex what sensuality is to romance!

Research has shown that certain smells or scents can arouse both sexes. For instance; women are supposedly aroused by the smell of cucumber, vanilla, musk, and banana bread. Men are aroused by the scent of pumpkin pie, cinnamon, vanilla, and lavender. Did you know that chocolate releases sexual hormones both in men and women? Bring on the chocolate!

Here are various food suggestions:

Apples	artichokes
asparagus	bananas
beef wellington	body jams
bouillabaisse	breads
cheese	brochettes
cupcakes	candy
caviar	cheesecake
cherries	chicken
chocolate	cookies
cornish game hen	cream puffs
crepe suzette	cucumber
duck a l'orange	eggs benedict
escargot	exotic salads
filet mignon	flambés
fondues	fruit salad
glazed carrots	grapes
green beans	palm hearts
honey	ice cream
lobster	melon
mousse	mussels
nuts	raw oysters
pasta	pastries
pate	pineapple
figs	prawns
prosciutto	pumpkin pie
rack of lamb	raspberries
rice pilaf	salmon wellington
shish kabobs	soufflés
strawberries	stuffed potatoes
sushi	tortes
truffles	waffles
watermelon	whipping cream

The presentation also plays a factor when you use food for romantic purposes. The two have always appeared to connect in an intimate dance of the senses.

Add sexy cocktail to your sensual culinary experience, here are a few suggestions:

- Between the Sheets
- Ménage à Trois
- Afternoon Delight
- Silk Panty Martini
- Sex on the Beach
- Full Monty Recipe
- Buttery Nipple
- Climax

Sweet Tasting Woman Martini

1 oz. Bacardi White Rum
1 oz. Malibu Rum
1 tablespoon coconut cream
2 ounce of club soda
5 large ice cubes in shaker

Add all ingredients in a martini shaker, shake 5 to 6 times.
Serve in a frosted martini glass (wet glass then put in the
freezer for 5-10 minutes).

TABLE SETTING FOR HOME DINING

Place  **Setting**

2 Dinner Plates
2 Salad Plates
2 Dinner Knives
2 Salad Forks
2 Soup Spoons
2 Dessert Spoons

2 Bread & Butter Plates
2 Cups and Saucers
2 Dinner Forks
2 Teaspoons
2 Dessert Forks
2 Water Glasses

2 Wine Glasses   2 Linen Napkins
1 Tablecloth or   2 Placemats

Setting Your Table for Dining:

- Place a placemat in front of each chair
- Place a service (dinner) plate on each placemat
- Left of the service plate, starting closest to the plate, place the dinner fork and the salad fork
- Right of the service plate, starting closest to the plate, place the dinner knife, the soup spoon and the teaspoon
- Top of the service plate position dessert fork or spoon or the appetizer fork, one pointing to the left and the other to the right
- Upper left of the service plate, place the bread & butter plate with the butter knife placed on the plate
- Upper right side of the service plate, place the cup and saucer
- Slightly right of center just above the cup and saucer, place the white wine glass
- Slightly left and above the white wine glass, place the red wine glass
- Slightly left and above the red wine glass place the water glass. The Soup Bowl or Salad Plate are placed on top of the service plate. Fold the napkin and place it under the fork area

DINING AMBIANCE

2	Roses of Petals
28	Tea-light Candles
1	Tall Vase
1	Rose with Greenery
1	White Placemat

Soft Room Lighting
Fireplace (if you have one)
Romantic Mood Music

- Place white placemat at the center of the table
- Place the 28 tea-light candles to form a heart shape
- Place the vase with rose and greenery in the center
- Sprinkle the rose petals around the outside of the heart
- Colour of the rose and rose petals would be your choice
- Recommended colour is either red or her favourite color
- No overhead lighting unless you have a dimmer
- Living room lighting should be soft
- Fireplace ignited or put on
- Place other tea-light candles in holders around the room
- Romantic mood music playing in the background
- Duration of music playlist should be at least 3 to 4 hours

Dinner music is one of your best tools for creating the ambiance for your guest or significant other. Remember music is to be kept in the background conversations need to predominate, so make sure it's not too loud.

Dinner party music shouldn't bother your guests. I received a bit of an education on this point recently when a dinner guest asked (very politely) if I could change the jazz music I had on. She said that she found the unresolved tension of the jazz chords distracting.

When I listened for a few minutes, I realized she had a point. I may love the music, but it was drawing attention to itself. I was wrong to assume that it worked well for a dinner party.

Soft classical music is always a right choice. If you choose music with singing, be careful to keep it low enough that people aren't trying to listen to the words instead of each other. Choosing your dinner music is something you can do well in advance.

WINE PAIRING

There are two items as guidelines for matching your food and wine: the weight and flavour of your culinary choice.

Weight for wines just refers to alcohol content:

- Light means about 8% to 10%
- Medium-bodied means about 10.5% to 12%
- Full-bodied means about 12.5% to 16%

The next consideration is the essence of your dish.

- The sweet fare should be matched with a sweet wine, ice or sparkling wine.
- The lighter delicate fare should be matched with an acidic wine, a white or rosé.
- The savory or robust fare should be matched with an intense red wine.

How much should I spend?

Some of the best wines I have tasted have been in the $25 to $40 range.

What kind of wine glasses should I use?

• Red wines are full-bodied in character; a large bowl shaped glass will allow it to breathe.
• White wine is cold and refreshing; a medium bowl shaped glass keeps it cool longer.
• Champagne is bubbly; Champagne flutes are tall and thin allowing the inspection of
colour, and movement of the bubbles. All wines should be served in a delicate type of stemware.

Temperature for Wine?

• Aged red wines: 16-17 °C
• Young Reds: 14-16 °C
• Rosés: 10-12 °C
• Whites: 8-10 °C
• Aged whites: 10-12 °C
• Sparkling wines: 7-10 °C
• Dessert wines: 7-8 °C
• Dry generous wines: 7 °C
• Ice wine best served at 12° C

If you chill wine much below these temperatures guidelines, you risk compromising both flavor and balance. Should I let the wine breathe? There is no need to let chilled white wines breathe you should open red wine about half an hour before serving or use a decanter or aerator. This allows the air to get in and bring out the bouquet and flavor. Should I serve the wine my guest brought?

The wine your guest brings is a gift; it is up to you whether to serve it or not. If you have carefully paired your fare and wine, then put it aside for another time. If you think your guest will be offended, you can always serve it before or after dinner. Selecting wines to complement your fare can be accomplished if you have the knowledge. Another suggestion, share the history of your wine choices with your guest/guests for their amusement and appreciation.

WHITE WINES:

Chardonnay:

• a green-skinned grape variety

• originated in the Burgundy wine region of eastern France

• is now grown from England to New Zealand

• tends to be medium to light body

• is an important component of many sparkling wines including Champagne

• pairs with fish/seafood, salads, soups, chicken, veal

Chablis wine

• a richness that is widely-planted and tends to reveal a California quality

• thrives in a variety of climates

• fruity and rich

• most popular

• in-demand grape varieties

• reliably pleasing flavours • pairs with a broad range of foods especially oysters, fish/seafood, sauces, dairy

Chenin Blanc:

• has been blended with honey and flowers

• high levels of acidity

- is grown in France, California, Australia, New Zealand, and South Africa
- absolutely delicious
- pairs with salads, soups, fish/seafood, chicken

Geürztraminer:

- deeply colored, full-flavored, highest alcohol content white wine in the world
- smells like roses and exotic fruits
- an abundance of flavour and richness
- appealing to lovers of big, bold wines
- wonderfully exuberant
- is grown in New Zealand, Washington State, Oregon, California and Australia
- pairs with spicy and boldly flavored dishes such as Chinese, Indian, Thai cuisines

Pinot Blanc:

- full-bodied, rich white wine
- is well-known and esteemed
- brilliantly crisp in flavour
- refreshing
- is grown in France, Austria, and Germany
- classic wine
- widely used for wine production
- is used extraordinarily well
- it is usually a blend to create a wonderfully opulent dessert wine
- pairs with Japanese cuisine, fish/seafood, salads

Pinot Gris (also called Pinot Grigio)

• two names for the same grape variety; first French, second Italian

• light and pleasantly acidic

• affordable and much-sought-after white wine

• a mutation of Pinot Noir

• subtle and slightly perfumed

• an excellent wine

• grown in Germany, Moravia, Romania, Slovenia, and Hungary

• also grown in California, Oregon, and New Zealand with excellent results

• pairs with bread, salads, soups, sauces, pasta, fish/seafood, pork, poultry

Riesling:

• most famous grape variety in Germany

• produces wine that ranges from dry to extremely sweet

• the alcohol level in German Riesling is reliably low

• made all over the world but famous and best grown in Germany

• a variety of styles

• sweet and expensive like dessert wines

• considered some of the best sweet wines in the world

• pairs with soup, fish/seafood, dairy, desserts, fruit/nuts, poultry, pork

Sauvignon Blanc:

• one of the two grape varieties blended to produce the famous white wines of Bordeaux the other grape variety is Semillon

• the grape variety is reliably fantastic

• great for the casual wine drinker

• Semillon was best known as a popular wine

• produced in France, Chile, New Zealand and Australia

• when aged, becomes additionally full-bodied and opulent

• Semillon blended with Sauvignon Blanc makes a drier white wine

• pairs with ethnic dishes like Chinese, Indian and Thai cuisines

Rhone & Blended Wines:

• the region of France is more well-known for red wines than whites

• exciting and delicious

• unique in the world of wine

• Condrieu is the most famous and respected white wine

• floral and redolent of apricots

• enjoyed when it is young

• Grenache Blanc is a lovely white wine

• produces a sparkling white wine that is excellent

• the region's most famous for their dessert wine

• pairs with Chinese cuisine, fish/seafood, poultry

Rosé, Sparkling, and Champagne:

• traditionally comes from France and Spain

• briskly acidic

• the rose colour is made by crushing red grapes and allowing their skins to remain in contact with the juice for a few hours or days; this turns the juice any colour from pink to copper

• a freshness most red wines do not have

• a weight that most white wines lack

• real rosé is wonderful

• wine with bubbles

• Champagne is the most famous sparkling wine

• from the Champagne region of France

• made from specific grapes

• produced according to a very strict method

• pairs with poultry, fish/seafood, summer type foods

RED WINES:

Shiraz/Syrah

• grown mostly in California but also in France and Australia

• Shiraz grape was once alleged to have originated in Persia

• a heavy red wine

• its spicy with peppery flavours

• such flavours are blackberry, plum, some licorice, and mocha

- rich and full
- should be served in a large bowl glass
- at a room temperature of 64°F – the warmest a red wine can be served
- Beef and hearty foods
- pairs with all spicy foods, Asian, Mexican cuisine

Beaujolais

- originally produced in the Beaujolais region of France
- the distinct winemaking process
- sugar is added to enhance the alcohol content
- it barely qualifies as a wine
- most Beaujolais should be drunk within two years of being bottled
- vintage up to 10 years
- light, fruity and easy to drink
- aromas of pear and banana
- pairs with poultry, pork, red sauce pasta, strong cheeses

Pinot Noir

- light red wine
- some experts consider this wine to be the finest in the world

- originally grown in France but now in California, Oregon, Australia, and New Zealand
- the grape is extremely difficult to grow
- has a range of colours from a cherry red to brown
- flavours of earth, vanilla, oak-infused with fruity flavours like raspberry, strawberry, and plum

- pairs with beef, pork, strong cheeses, red sauce pasta, goose, wild game

Merlot

- name of the grape
- grown in France, California, and Chile
- not well suited for long aging
- mellow in complexity
- an easy drinking wine
- flavours of black cherry, plum, orange, and violets
- an excellent complement to chocolate
- pairs with beef, hearty dishes, strong cheeses, chicken, red sauce, pasta

Cabernet Sauvignon

- name of the grape
- one of the world's most famous wines
- has a depth of complexity and a richness of flavour
- South America, Australia, Lebanon, California, Canada, and France
- mellow, hearty, mild and yet has a richness of flavour
- primary taste of black currant with overtones of blackberry and mint
- traditionally aged in oak, so it takes on an oak vanilla-like flavour as well
- served in a large glass bowl
- pairs with beef, lamb, goose, cheeses, red sauce pasta, chocolate

Red Zinfandel

- originated in Italy is currently primarily grown in California

- grown on the coastline

- colour ranges from deep red to bordering black

- spicy and peppery with a hint of fruity flavours of berries

- narrow mouth glass

- served at room temperature

- can be served within a year or two

- when aged, the flavour is quite mellow

- red skins color the wine red (without it becomes white)

- pairs with fast food, beef, strong cheeses

PORT

- Port originates from the Porto area, in the Douro Valley of Portugal

- Port first became popular when the English were at war with France

- the term "Port" can only refer to these wines one of the more famous of the fortified wines

- there are 48 authorized grape varieties which can go into a port

- pairs with strong cheese, fruit, and chocolate

Note: When pairing wine with Soup just remember the texture of the broth and the heartiness of the ingredients, the heartier or creamy the soup you pair with the same type of texture of wine.

1. White Wines – a light wine that is well-adapted for a simple an delicate style of food (such as salads or fish) and a velvety consistency (such as a creamy or roasted poultry dish).

2. Red Wines – a social type almost fruity in taste for conversation or while eating an uncomplicated meal or appetizer. It is a tantalizing wine with a whisper of intensity to pair with the red meat dishes such as lamb, beef, etc..

3. Champagne, Sparkling or Rosé – just for those special unpretentious moments when one wishes to set a romantic ambiance.

4. After Dinner Wine – a silky smooth Port that can be served with cheeses, fruits, and nuts or passionate, sweet Ice Wine that can pair with a dessert that best suits the palate of both you and your guest.

FOOD PORTIONS

GUY   **WOMAN**

Appetizers before dinner

• 4-7   2-4

Appetizers for dinner

• 10-12   6-8

Entrée Servings

10 oz	Meat/Fish	6 oz
1 lb.	Ribs	½ lb.
3-4 cups	Soup/Stew	1-2 cups
2 cups	Grains	1 cup
1 large	Potato	1 medium
1-2 serving	Vegetables	1 serving
2-3 serving	Pasta (side)	1-2 serving
3-4 cups	Pasta (entrée)	2-3 cups
2 cups	Salad	1 cup
2-3 pieces	Bread	1-2 pieces

Desserts

1 large slice	Cake/Pie	1 small slice
3 Scoops	Ice Cream	1-2 scoops
3-4 Scoops	Fruit	1-2 scoops

The Fare order of a formal 5 course sit down dinner is the following: Starter–Soup–Salad–Entree–Dessert

Whether it is the cocktail hour or sharing indulgence, this is a sensual opportunity to feed each other. The option is to serve bread and salad with the Sharing Indulgence.

DINNER CENTERPIECE

You need to learn a few simple skills to produce beautiful table arrangements consistently. Start with these tips for all your dinner table arrangements:

• An arrangement that looks good from all sides of the dinner table for your guests to admire.

• An arrangement about five inches or lower, so guests can easily see over it.

• Don't put highly scented flowers on the dinner table because their aroma can complete with the food aromas and a guest may be allergic to the strong scent as well.

• White taper candles are dramatic; tea candles are more subtle yet both lovely.

If you can master three tried-and-true arrangements for your dinner parties, you can always produce eye candy for your table. Later, as you become more practiced and at ease with the routine of planning a dinner party (whether for one or several couples), you can add more arrangements to your repertoire. But for now, let's concentrate on three arrangements. With just those three, you can cover almost every dinner party you give over a year.

Arrangement 1: A simple white table centerpiece arrangement; choose white flowers and some simple foliage. Arrange it in a vase making sure it is either clear or white as well.

Arrangement 2: A table centerpiece with a touch of drama. Choose a colour with some oomph to it, no pastels this time; pick from a seductive purple. A radiant yellow-gold, or a majestic blue. You can pump up the drama very easily if you have plates or napkins of the same colour.

Arrangement 3: The "emergency" table centerpiece. Stress-free and inexpensive, these table centerpieces will do the job for you every time you need a quick solution to the no-flowers table centerpiece problem.

Use your imagination:

• Clear vase or bowl of small lemons or limes, or a combination.

- Bowl with a variety of fruits with dry leaves strewn around it.
- Different size glasses with colored water placed on a mirror with a floating candle in each glass.
- Vase with an array of colorful dry beans and some extra sprinkled around the vase with an assortment of candles.
- Wine bottles with taper candles in them and different colour ribbons tied around the neck of the bottle.

Another idea when you're making her dinner, do a themed centerpiece that speaks of her. For instance, if she plays golf: like a tall clear vase filled with golf balls then add water and place a floating candle, place stem-free flowers around the base

A ROMANTIC AFFARE

A romantic dinner for two in the privacy of your home, both of you can go shopping; then together cook an orgasmic culinary dinner with a romantic ambiance.

MENU:

Prawn Stuffed Avocado
Honey Citrus Chicken Breasts
Roasted Potatoes
Buttered Dill Baby Carrots
Chocolate Dipped Strawberries
Wine

Shopping List:

2 Chicken Breasts

3 Large Oranges
100 ml Parsley (dried)
100 ml Garlic (dried minced)
200 ml Onion (dried minced)
1 Bunch Cilantro (fresh)
1 Bunch Dill (fresh)
6 Large Prawns
1 large Avocado
1 Celery
1 Red Onion
Dijon mustard
1 Habanero Chile
Mayonnaise
1 Lemon
2 Russet Potatoes
1 Bunch of Baby Carrots
1 Package of Mixed Greens
1 Package of Fresh Strawberries
1 cup Chocolate Melting Chips
Butter
Seasoning Salt
Honey
Wine of Choice

Refer to: Wine Pairing to choose your wines that pairs well with your dinner.

Refer to: How to set a Romantic Table for Two in order to set your table.

Refer to: Setting a Romantic Ambiance for Dinner to set the ambiance for the evening

Suggestions:

• Confirm with her that she doesn't have any food allergies before shopping.

- Arrival time is 7:00 PM dinner should be 7:30 PM although you can be flexible.
- Dress in a suit.
- If dating do not use the heart candle arrangement, arrange the candles in a circle instead.

Prep Time: 10-15 minutes
Cooking Time: N/A

Prawn Stuffed Avocado

1 cup	Prawns (cut in halves)
1 large	Avocado's (cut into eighths)
½ cup	Celery (finely diced)
1/4 cup	Red Onion (finely diced)
1 head	Butter Lettuce

Cilantro Aioli Sauce:

1 tbsp.	Dijon mustard
1 tbsp.	Honey
¼ cup	Cilantro
1 tsp.	Habanero Chile (minced)
1 cup	Mayonnaise
1 tsp.	Lemon Juice

1. Peeled and cut prawns in half
2. Cook Prawns until pink then cool
3. Cut Avocado in half and remove pit
4. Take knife and square avocado into eighths   (don't cut into the avocado shell)
5. Remove avocado squares from the shell
6. Add avocado, prawns, celery and red onion in a bowl
7. Add all ingredients for sauce in a blender and blend at high speed
8. Add half of the sauce to the bowl and toss gently until all is coated
9. Spoon mixture into avocado shell
10. Chopped Lettuce, rinse and place around avocado
11. Refrigerate until ready to serve

12. Drizzle remaining sauce on lettuce

Prep Time: 5-10 minutes
Cooking Time: 20-25 minutes

Honey Citrus Chicken

2	Chicken Breasts
1 cup	Squeezed Orange Juice
¼ cup	Honey
1 tbsp.	Garlic
1 tbsp.	Onion
1 tsp.	Parsley
½ tbsp.	Seasoning Salt

1. Mix the orange juice & honey in a bowl
2. Add chicken and toss to coat
3. Sprinkle Garlic, Onion and Seasoning salt
4. Bake in preheated oven at 375 degrees for 20 minutes

Prep Time: 10 minutes
Cooking Time: 35 to 45 minutes

Roasted Potatoes

2 large	Potatoes
1 cup	Butter (melted)
1 tsp.	Minced Onion
1 tsp.	Seasoning Salt

1. Peel and cut potatoes into eighths, place in open baking dish
2. Pour butter or margarine over the potatoes
3. Sprinkle the onion and salt over potatoes
4. Put potatoes in a 350-degree oven for 45 minutes
5. Potatoes have to be crispy on the outside to be ready

Prep Time: 5 minutes
Cooking Time: 15 minutes

Buttered Dill Baby Carrots

1 bunch	Baby Carrots
½ cup	Melted Butter
¼ cup	Dill (chopped)

1. Wash and peel carrots
2. Steam carrots until tender
3. Add butter & dill
4. Toss and Serve

Prep Time: 10 minutes
Cooking Time: 10 to 15 minutes

Chocolate coated Strawberries

1 dozen	Strawberries (large)
1 cup	Milk or White Chocolate
Wax Paper	

1. Wash strawberries and dry completely
2. Melt the chocolate in a stainless steel bowl over a pot of steaming water
3. Keep stirring until completely melted
4. Immediately dip strawberries in chocolate to coat
5. Place on wax paper until harden

TWILIGHT PICNIC

In a beautiful park or Oceanside setting that will take her breath away, romance is a priority.

What you will need for the picnic:

1	Blanket
2	Wine Glasses

1	Bottle of Champagne
1	Cock Screw
2	Plates
2	Napkins
3	Appetizers
1	Musician

Shopping List:

1 bunch	Green Onions
3 sticks	Celery
1 large	Tomato
1 large	Jalapeno Pepper
2 large	Avocado
2 large	Lemons
2 large	Limes
1 bunch	Fresh Cilantro
1 small	Sour Cream
1 Large Jar	Salsa
1 can	Kidney Beans
2 can	Black Olives (sliced)
1 package	Cheddar Cheese
100 ml	Chili Flakes
12	Large Prawns
½ lb.	Fresh Scallops
1 bottle	Olive Oil
¼ cup	Cajun Spice
¼ cup	Paprika
¼ cup	Parsley (dried)
¼ cup	Seasoning Salt
¼ cup	Garlic (dried minced)
¼ cup	Onion (dried minced)
1 bag	Nachos
1 package	Skewer Sticks
1 package	Napkins
1 bottle	Wine

• The Picnic at a park; you select close to where she lives.
• Hire a Musician that will play mood music on their instrument.
• Set the time to about 1 ½ to 2 hours before sunset.

• Have the musician arrive 10 minutes after her arrival.
• Plan to have her meet you at the park to watch the sunset.
• If you tell her to be there at 7:00 PM, plan to arrive there 15 minutes before.
• Order & pick up the food or have a caterer bring the food to the location.
• Have the picnic set up just before her arrival.
• Once she arrives and sees what you have planned, allow enough time to express her surprise and excitement.
• Sit on the blanket and serve the champagne; feed her an item of the finger food.
• Make sure the musician texts you before arriving so that his timing is perfect.
• Have her close her eyes in anticipation to keep it a surprise. Don't let her open her eyes until the music starts.

Menu:

Scallop Ceviche
Mexicana Layer Dip
Cajun Prawns on a Stick

Prep Time: 10 minutes
Cooking Time: 7 to 10 minutes

The Mexicana Layer Dip

2 cups	Kidney Beans
1 cup	Black Olives (sliced)
4 large	Green Onion (diced)
2 cup	Sour Crème
2 cups	Avocado (thinly sliced)
2 cups	Salsa
3 cups	Cheddar Cheese (grated)
1 tbsp.	Chili Flakes

1. Layer each item starting with kidney beans ending with chili flakes - top to bottom in a square deep dish
(6 x 6)
2. Refrigerate up to an hour or even overnight (optional)

Prep Time: 5 minutes
Cooking Time: 5 to 7 minutes

Cajun Prawns on a Stick

12	large Prawns
¼ cup	Olive Oil
2 tbsp.	Lemon Juice
1 tbsp.	Cajun Spice
1 tsp.	Paprika
1 tsp.	Parsley (dried)
1 tsp.	Seasoning Salt
1 tsp.	Garlic (dried minced)
1 tsp.	Onion (dried minced)

4 Skewer Sticks (soaked for 20 minutes)

1. Add all the above ingredients (except shrimp) in a bowl and mix well
2. Toss the prawns into mixture and marinate in fridge up to ½ hour
3. Put three prawns on each skewer. You can either barbecue or roast in a preheated oven at 350F until pink.

Prep Time: 20 minutes
Marinating Time: 4 to 5 hours

Scallop Ceviche

½ lb.	Fresh Scallops (diced)
1 tbsp.	Jalapeno (minced)
1 cup	Tomato (diced)
¼ cup	Green Onions (chopped)
¼ cup	Celery (diced)
Juice	3 Limes
1 large	Avocado (diced)
¼ cup	Fresh Cilantro (chopped)

1. Prepare all above ingredients as instructed
2. Put all ingredients in a bowl and toss well
3. Refrigerate for 4 to 5 hours
4. Tossing every 1/2 hour

ITALIAN MY LOVE

MENU:

Personalized Heart Shaped Pizza

Shopping List:

1 package	Pillsbury Pizza Crust
1 can	Pizza Sauce
1 can	Ripe Olives
1 lb.	Mozzarella Cheese
1 large	Red Pepper
1 large	Green Pepper
1 cup	Pepperoni slices

Prep Time: 10 to 15 minutes
Cooking Time: 15 to 17 minutes

The Pizza

1. Heat oven to 425°F for classic crust or 400°F for thin crust
2. Remove dough from package
3. Roll out with a thickness you prefer on a floured counter
4. Form dough into a heart
5. Place on greased baking sheet
6. Apply the sauce
7. Grate and sprinkle on the cheese
8. Finely dice the red pepper, green pepper, olives and mushrooms
9. With scissors shaped pepperoni into hearts then place on pizza's
10. Spell each letter of her/his name with the variety of toppings you have prepared.

C	red pepper
R	green pepper
Y	mushrooms
S	olives
T	red pepper
A	green pepper
L	olives

Put into oven and bake classic crust 10 to 12 minutes, thin crust 8 to 10 minutes or until cheese bubbles and the crust has browned.

You can also make mini pizza's with a each letter of her/his name and then serve on a long platter and serve with champagne.

THE HEARTY BRUNCH

A romantic brunch has a lasting effect and appreciation. The breakfast is prepared in hearts from eggs to bacon and pancakes. Top this with a fresh cup of robust coffee and a tantalizing mimosa. Start the bacon first and while that is cooking in the oven, you can prepare the eggs and pancakes.

MENU:

Heart Shaped Cheese Omelet
Heart Shaped Bacon
Heart Shaped Pancakes

Shopping List:

1 dozen	Large Eggs
1 bunch	Green Onions
1 small	Red Pepper
1 lb.	Bacon
1 box	Pancake Mix

1 brick	Butter
1 bottle	Maple Syrup
1 bottle	Ketchup
1 can	Oil Spray
Small	Milk or Cream
Small	Cheddar Cheese
2 large	Heart Shaped Cookie Cutter
1 large	Russet Potato
1 small	Onion
2 tbsp.	Canola Oil
1 tbsp.	Seasoning Salt

Prep Time: 10 minutes
Cooking Time: 12 to 15 minutes

Heart-shaped Bacon

8-10 slices	Bacon (Cookie Sheet with Rims)

1. Preheat your oven to 400 degrees
2. Lay bacon flat lengthwise
3. Cut strip in half
4. Each slice has to be 5 inches long
5. Take bacon slice and folded it in half lengthwise
6. Take two of the slices (each being one side of the heart) and shape into a heart on the cookie sheet
7. Bake for 15 to 20 minutes
8. Place on plate

Prep Time: 10 minutes
Cooking Time: 5 to 7 minutes

Heart Shaped Mini Omelet

4 Large	Eggs
1 tbsp.	Green Onion (chopped)
¼ cup	Red Pepper (diced)
¼ cup	Mushrooms (diced)
¼ cup	Milk
¼ cup	Cheddar Cheese (shredded)
½ tsp.	Seasoning Salt

2   Heart Shaped Cookie Cutters

1. Saute vegetables until soften
2. Whisk eggs, milk, cheese & seasoning salt
3. Add sauté vegetables to egg mixture
4. Spray frying pan & rings with cooking oil
5. Pour egg mixture into cutters
6. Remove cookie cutter once the egg mixture is set about 15 seconds
7. Cover & cook over low heat until set (3-5 minutes)

Prep Time: 10 minutes
Cooking Time: 12 to 15 minutes

Heart-shaped Pancakes

1 Box   Pancake Mix
1 tsp.   Cinnamon powder
2   Heart-shaped Cookie Cutter

1. Follow directions on pancake box and add cinnamon
2. Add cinnamon to pancake mix and blend
4. Spray frying pan & cutters with cooking oil
5. Place cookie cutter in pan
6. Pour the pancake mix in cookie cutter
7. Remove cookie cutter once the pancake mix bubbles
8. Flip the pancake and cook for a minute or so
9. Continue this process with each pancake

Serve with condiments; maple syrup, butter, ketchup and maybe some fresh fruit like sliced strawberries.

Prep Time: 5 minutes
Cooking Time: 15-20 minutes

Pan Fried Potatoes

1 large   Russet Potato (diced)
1 small   Onion (chopped)

1. Use non-stick frying pan

2. Add oil, potatoes, and onion
3. Let brown on one side before turning
4. Continue the process until fries on crisp and soft in the center

A FARE CHANCE MINI COOKBOOK

VOLUME CONVERSIONS (approximately)

Imperial	Metric
1/4 teaspoon (tsp.)	1.25 milliliter (ml)
1/2 tsp.	2.5 ml
1 tsp.	5.0 ml
1 tablespoon (tbsp.)	18 ml
1/4 cup	71 ml
1/3 cup	95 ml
1/2 cup	142 ml
2/3 cup	189 ml
3/4 cup	213 ml
1 cup	284 ml
1 1/2 cups	426 ml
1 2/3 cups	473 ml
1 3/4 cups	497 ml
2 cups	568 ml
4 cups	1 liter
½ ounce (oz.)	14 grams (g)
1 oz.	28 g
2 oz.	57 g
3 oz.	85 g
4 oz.	113 g
6 oz.	170 g
7 oz.	198 g
8 oz.	227 g
9 oz.	255 g
10 oz.	284 g
12 oz.	340 g
1 pound (lb.)	500 g
1½ lbs.	750 g

Fahrenheit	Celsius	Oven Heat
225°	110°	very low
250°	120°	very low
275°	135°	low
300°	150°	low
325°	165°	moderate warm
350°	175°	medium
375°	190°	moderately hot
400°	205°	hot
425°	220°	hot
450°	230°	very hot
500°	260°	extreme hot

MORE RECIPES TO CREATE A DINNER MENU

Prep Time: 10 minutes
Cooking Time: N/A

Cucumber & Green Onion Salad

1	English Cucumber (sliced)
3	Green Onions (chopped)
	Cucumber Dressing (below)

1. Add all the above ingredients in a bowl & toss
2. Best when refrigerate for ½ hour

Cucumber Dressing

½ Cup	Sour Cream
1 tbsp.	Mayonnaise
1 tsp.	Malt Vinegar
1 tsp.	Dill Weed (dry) or 2 tbsps. fresh dill
½ tsp.	Seasoning Salt

Put above ingredients in bowl and mix

Prep Time: 15 minutes
Cooking Time: N/A

Cauliflower & Red Pepper Salad

3 cups	Cauliflower (chopped)
1 large	Red Pepper (sliced)
1 small	White Onion (sliced)
1 cup	Creamy Dressing

1. Add all above ingredients in a bowl and toss
2. Put in fridge for up to 1 or 2 hours

Creamy Dressing

1 cup	Mayonnaise
1 tbsp.	White Vinegar
1 tsp.	Pepper
½ tsp.	Seasoning Salt

Prep Time: 15 minutes
Cooking Time: 35 to 60 minutes
Serve with: French bread

Lobster Chowder

1 lb.	Lobster Meat
5 large	Russet Potatoes (diced)
1 large	Carrot (sliced)
1 med	Onion (diced)
¼ cup	Butter
1 can	Consommé Soup
2 cups	Chicken Stock (Powder)
1 can	Tomato Paste
3 Cups	Cream
1 cup	White Wine
2	Bay Leafs
1 tsp.	Thyme
1 tsp.	Seasoning Salt

1. Melt butter, add onions and cook until tender

2. Add consommé, chicken stock, potatoes, carrots; seasonings cook until tender
3. Whisk tomato paste and white wine
4. Add crème, lobster, stir and let simmer for 1 hour

Prep Time: 20 minutes
Cooking Time: 60 minutes
Serve with: French bread

Chick Pea Soup

2 cans	Chick Peas
1 med.	Onion (diced)
1 large	Potato (diced)
1 tbsp.	Garlic (minced)
4 cans	Chicken Broth or Vegetable Stock
½ cup	Crème
1 tbsp.	Parsley (dry)
To taste	Salt & Pepper

1. Add all the above except crème & parsley to a pot
2. Put on high heat until boiling then turn to low and cover for 30 minutes
3. Put in blender until creamy then add back into pot
4. Add cream and parsley, salt & pepper
5. Heat until bubbling then serve

Prep Time: 5 to 10 minutes
Cooking Time: 20 minutes
Serve with: Meat Entrée & Vegetable

Cheese Mashed Potatoes

2 medium	Russet Potatoes
1 tbsp.	Cream Cheese
1 tbsp.	Mayonnaise
2 tsp.	Butter
½ cup	Milk
2 tbsp.	Parmesan Cheese
1 tsp.	Garlic (dry minced)
2 tsp.	Seasoning Salt

1 tsp.	Parsley (dry)
1 tsp.	Basil (dry)
1 tsp.	Onion (dry minced)

1. Wash potatoes, peel or leave skins on, your preference
2. Boiled potatoes
3. Mashed the potatoes
4. Add remaining ingredients, mix and serve

Prep Time: 15 minutes
Cooking Time: 2 hours
Serve with: Ham & Vegetable

Scallop Potatoes

4 large	Russet Potatoes (peeled & sliced)
1 med	Cooking Onions (sliced)
1 lb.	Mozzarella Cheese (sliced)
1 lb.	Swiss Cheese (sliced)
1 cup	Parmesan Cheese (grated)
2 cups	Milk or Crème
½ cup	Butter or Margarine (melted)
To taste	Seasoning Salt

1. Layer potatoes in pan then layer onions & sprinkle cheeses to cover
2. Another layer of potatoes & onions
3. Pour milk and butter over potatoes, cover with tin foil
4. Put into oven at 375° for 1 ½ hours or until potatoes are tender
5. Discard tin foil and layer the cheeses again on top of potatoes
6. Put back into oven for 30 minutes or until cheese is melted and golden

Prep Time: 5 minutes
Cooking Time: 10 to 15 minutes
Serve with: Pork Chops & Vegetable

Chinese Fried Rice

2 cups	Minute Rice
5 strips	Bacon (chopped)
1 medium	Onion (diced)
1 cup	Frozen Peas
4 large	Mushrooms (thinly sliced)
2 cups	Water
3 tbsp.	Soya Sauce

1. Fry bacon and then crumble
2. Fry onion & mushrooms
3. Boil water & soya sauce
4. When water comes to a boil add rice and vegetables
5. Cover for 10 to 15 minutes

Prep Time: 25 minutes
Cooking Time: 25 to 35 minutes
Serve with: Salad

Paella

3 cups	Minute Rice (uncooked)
4	Chicken Wings (separated)
1	Italian Sausage (sliced)
6	Prawns
6	Frozen Kiwi Mussels
½ pkg.	Mix Seafood
½ med	Red Pepper (finely sliced)
½ med	Green Pepper (finely sliced)
1 medium	Onion (finely sliced)
1 cup	Frozen Peas
1/2 cup	Salsa
2 cups	Chicken Broth
1 cup	White Wine
½ cup	Olive Oil
½ cup	Butter

| 1 tbsp. | Turmeric |

1. Roast chicken wings in oven at 350 until golden
2. Fry peppers, onion and sausage in olive oil
3. Add all the ingredients except for mussels into a shallow baking pan and toss
4. Lay mussels face down into the rice mixture and cover with tin foil
5. Put in 350˚ preheated oven for 25-35 minutes then serve immediately

Prep Time: 5 minutes
Cooking Time: 10 minutes
Serve with: Fish & Rice

Stir Fry Zucchini Mix

1 large	Zucchini (quartered & sliced)
1 med	White Onion (sliced)
4 large	White Mushrooms
3 tbsp.	Butter (melted)
1 tsp.	Seasoning Salt

1. Place zucchini, mushrooms, and onion into melted butter
2. Season & Stir fry until tender and golden

Prep Time: 15 minutes
Cooking Time: 30 to 40 minutes
Serve with: Meat Entre & Potato Side

Roasted Vegetables

1 cup	Celery Root (peeled & cubed)
1 cup	Hubbard Squash (peeled & cubed)
1 cup	Green & Red Pepper (quartered)
2 cups	Beets (cooked & quartered)
5 large	Mushrooms (halved)
1 large	Onion (quartered)
3 large	Cloves of Garlic
½ cup	Olive Oil

½ cup	Balsamic Dressing
¼ cup	Cilantro (chopped finely)
¼ cup	Basil (chopped finely)
½ cup	Parmesan Cheese (grated)

1. Preheat oven at 400 °
2. Place all the above vegetables on cookie sheet
3. Add oil, vinegar, garlic, salt, and toss until coated
4. Put into for 30 to 40 minutes or until just tender

Prep Time: 30 minutes
Cooking Time: 60 minutes
Serve with: Salad & Baguette

Vegetarian Lasagna

6 strips	Lasagna Noodles
½ cup	Zucchini (sliced)
½ cup	Mushrooms (sliced)
½ cup	Green Pepper (diced)
1 stalk	Celery (diced)
1 cup	Carrot (thinly sliced)
1 cup	Onions (thinly sliced)
1 cup	Diced Tomatoes
½ pkg.	Frozen Spinach
2 cups	Mozzarella Cheese (grated)
1 cup	Parmesan Cheese
1 cup	Pizza Sauce
2 cups	Spaghetti Sauce
1 tbsp.	Garlic (dry minced)
1 tbsp.	Parsley (dry)
2 tbsp.	Seasoning Salt
1	6 x 8 Bread Pan

1. Cook lasagna noodles as per packaged instructions, cool and set aside
2. Toss the cheeses together in a separate bowl
3. Thaw spinach and squeeze excess water out of spinach until dry
4. Cook all vegetables lightly and cool

5. Add the spinach and tomatoes to cooked vegetables and toss
6.   The add the sauces, garlic, parsley, and salt to vegetables and toss
7.   Spread vegetable mixture on bottom on lasagna pan
8.   Layer with noodles (two strips each layer)
9.   Layer with vegetable mixture onto noodles
10. Layer the cheeses over the vegetable mixture about 2 ½ cups
11. Continue pattern for two more layers
12. Top with the remaining 3 cups of cheese mixture
13. Cover with foil and place in oven at 375 for 45 minutes
14. Uncover and cook for another 15 minutes

Prep Time: 5 minutes
Cooking Time: 15 to 20 minutes
Serve with: Caesar Salad & French Bread

Escargot in White Wine Sauce Linguini

½ pkg.	Linguini Pasta
1 can	Escargot
½ cup	Flour
½ cup	Butter
2 cups	Cream
1 cup	White Wine
¼ tsp.	Garlic (minced)
½ cup	Parmesan Cheese (grated)

1. Make pasta as per package instructions
2. Melt butter then add flour to saucepan making a paste on medium heat
3. Add the cream, wine, and garlic whisking until thicken (if it gets too thick add more crème)
4. Add Escargot and simmer for about 5 to 10 minutes stirring often
5. Once pasta is cook then drain
6. Place pasta on plate add sauce
7. Sprinkle with cheese

Prep Time: 10 minutes
Cooking Time: 20 to 25 minutes
Serve with: Rice & Salad

Baked Lemon Garlic Salmon

4 medium	Salmon (serving size)
½ cup	Butter (melted)
½ cup	White Wine
¼ cup	Lemon Juice
1 tbsp.	Garlic (minced)
1 tbsp.	Onion (minced)
To taste	Seasoning Salt

1. Put salmon pieces in tin foil
2. Mix all the other ingredients other than salt
3. Pour over salmon
4. Season with seasoning salt
5. Place in oven at 350° for 20 minutes or Barbeque although you should check the salmon because the bake time might alter due to thickness.

Prep Time: 5 minutes
Cooking Time: 5 to 7 minutes
Serve with: Rice & Salad

Curry Prawns

16 large	Prawns (shelled & halved)
1 large	Onion (chopped)
1 large	Red Pepper (sliced thinly)
1 large	Green Pepper (sliced thinly)
2 stalks	Celery (chopped)
1 tbsp.	Ginger (chopped)
1 tbsp.	Garlic (minced)
1 cup	White Wine
2 cups	Chicken Broth
2 cups	Crème
4 tbsp.	Butter (melted)
4 tbsp.	Curry Powder
2 tbsp.	White Sugar

3 tbsp.   Flour

1. Place butter and vegetables in a heated shallow pot
2. Cook all vegetables until tender
3. Add all dry ingredients and mix until thick paste forms
4. Then add the broth and wine then whisk vigorously until thickens
5. Add crème, whisk until thickens turn to low to med
6. Add shrimp and toss until pink then serve over rice

Prep Time: 10 minutes
Cooking Time: 20 to 30 minutes
Serve with: Fried Rice & Oriental Vegetable Mix

Pork Tid-Bits

2	Pork Boneless Steaks (cubed)
2	Eggs (whisked)
3 tbsp.	Soya Sauce
4 Cups	Canola Oil
2 Cups	Flour
1 tbsp.	Granulated Garlic
2 tbsp.	Seasoning Salt

1. Add soya and garlic to egg mix then add pork to egg mixture and coat
2. Put flour in a Ziploc bag and coat pork with flour
3. Shake excess flour off pork then add to oil and deep fry
4. Place in hot oil (use popcorn kernels to test the oil for readiness, once the kernels pop you know the oil is ready.
5. Then place on a paper towel, season with seasoning salt, granulated garlic
6. Place into roasting pan and put in a 350˚ preheated oven 20 minutes

Prep Time: 10 minutes
Cooking Time: 45 minutes
Serve with: Salad

Pan Fried Chicken Stew

6 Large	Chicken thighs
3 large	Carrots (peeled & quartered)
3 large	Potatoes (peeled & quartered)
1 large	Onion (quartered)
3 slices	Bacon (chopped)
1 tbsp.	Garlic (minced)
3 Cups	Water

1. Cook bacon then remove in frying pan until crisp
2. Remove & crumble then put aside
3. Place chicken pieces skin down in frying pan and cook until you can the chicken releases
4. Turn and cook on the other side for about 3 minutes
5. Place all the vegetables and bacon around chicken then pour in water
6. Season, cover and put on low to med for about 45 minutes
7. If you think the liquid is too low add a little more

Prep Time: 10 minutes
Cooking Time: 20 minutes
Serve with: Rice or Pasta

Beef & Tomato Combo

2 lb.	Ground Beef
1 large	Onion (diced)
1 large can	Tomatoes (diced)
1 tsp.	Garlic (minced)

1. Cook beef until brown
2. Cook the onions & mushrooms until tender and add to meat
3. Add the garlic and tomatoes to meat and turn to medium heat and cook until bubbling then serve

Prep Time: 20 minutes
Cooking Time: 45 minutes
Serve with: A Salad

Stuffed Green Peppers

1 lb.	Ground Meat (beef, chicken or lamb)
1 medium	Onion (diced)
2 large	Mushrooms (sliced)
2 large	Green Peppers
1 cup	*Rice (long grain)
1 can	Cheese or Celery Soup
1 cup	White Wine
2 tbsp.	Garlic (dry minced)
½ tsp.	Chili Pepper Flakes
1 tsp.	Seasoning Salt

1. Add the garlic, chili flakes, and salt to liquid for the rice and cook rice
2. Cut top off green peppers, clean inside, rinse and pat dry
3. Cook onions, mushrooms and meat then add to cooked rice and toss
4. Stuff rice and meat mixture into green pepper and put on cookie sheet
5. Bake in oven at 350° for 45 minutes or until tender
6. Add wine to soup and whisk over medium heat until hot
7. Pour over peppers just before serving

*Cook rice per package instructions.

Prep Time: 10-15 minutes
Cooking Time: 3 to 5 minutes
Served with: Wine

Stuffed Mushrooms

6 medium	Mushrooms (washed and pat dry)
1 cup	Bacon (cooked & crumbled)
1 cup	Smoked Cheese (grated)
1 pkg.	Cream Cheese (room temperature)

1 tbsp.	Onion (minced)
1 tbsp.	Garlic (minced)
1 tbsp.	Butter (melted)

1. Remove stem from mushroom then wash and pat dry
2. Place on cookie sheet
3. Bake in preheated oven @ 350° for 10 to 15 minutes
4. Remove mushrooms from oven, cool & pat dry again
5. Fry bacon, cool and crumble and set aside
6. Grate smoke cheese and add to crème cheese
7. Diced mushroom stems
8. Stir fry mushroom stems, onion and garlic until soft
9. Add bacon, mushroom, onion and garlic to cheese mix
10. Fill mushrooms with cheese mixture
11. Place under broiler until cheese turns golden

www.theguyedbook.com

76860004R00088

Made in the USA
Columbia, SC
15 September 2017